MOVIES AS
SOCIAL CRITICISM

Aspects of Their Social Psychology

by
I.C. JARVIE

The Scarecrow Press, Inc.
Metuchen, N.J. & London
1978

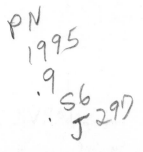

Library of Congress Cataloging in Publication Data

Jarvie, Ian C
    Movies as social criticism.

    Bibliography: p.
    Includes index.
    1. Moving-pictures--Social aspects. 2. Moving-
pictures--Psychological aspects. I. Title.
PN1995.9.S6J297   301.5'7   77-26778
ISBN 0-8108-1106-5

This book is dedicated
to L. A.

Let us not then attribute to the
stage a power of changing opinion
or manners, when it has only that
of following or heightening them.

--Jean-Jacques Rousseau, A Letter ...
Concerning the Effects of Theatrical
Entertainment on the Manners of Man-
kind (London, 1759).

CONTENTS

v

LIST OF ILLUSTRATIONS

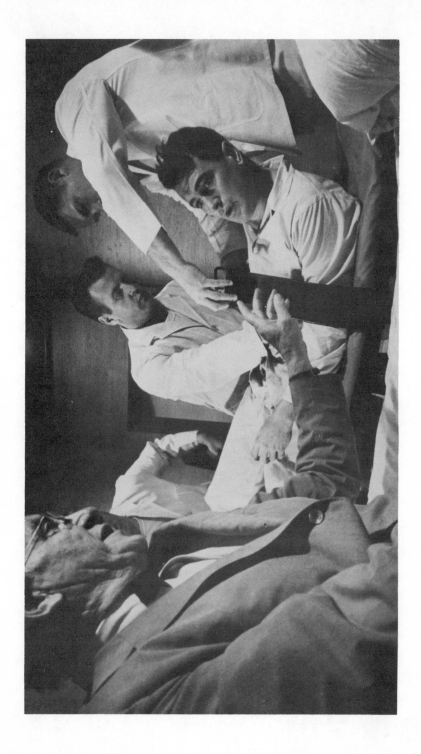

PREFACE

For far too long, movies were dismissed as social pap--mere popular entertainment. By titling this book Movies as Social Criticism I indicate my dissent from this summary dismissal. Popular movies are a rich source of ideas about, information (to be sure, misinformation also) concerning, and criticism of, society. By and large, their makers do not intend them to be sources of information and criticism. But the unintended consequences of social phenomena are very interesting. Creators in every field never cease to be surprised at the way their work is interpreted by the public. One of America's greatest filmmakers, John Ford, was quite scornful of critics who regarded him as a poet. Once finished, movies take on an existence independent of their creators. Popular movies were made for money and entertainment. This does not mean they will not reward careful sociological analysis.

No one ever intended movies to be important. They began as an obscure invention thrust into social prominence by businessmen intent on making money. Their unintended social significance stems from, among others, the fact that they tell stories; stories convey information and ideas; information and ideas affect the way people act; and stories meld people together into audiences--this too affects the way they act. The social consequences of being an audience are most important and usually underrated.

Opposite: Perhaps the most deeply and bitterly critical film of the sixties was John Frankenheimer's almost unnoticed masterpiece, Seconds. A wealthy middle-aged man, bored with life, is offered a second chance at youth and vocation. But technology offers no comfort for human failure, and he demands a third chance. Unfortunately, the company does not like failure, and in this horrifying scene Rock Hudson realizes he has been released to the Cadaver Procurement Section for disposal. Will Geer offers him the unction of the corporate motto: "Remember the dream, son...." The Paramount release was scripted by Lewis John Carlino.

When movies entered our society, that society was, as it almost always is, changing; as a consequence, movies, besides fulfilling new social functions, also competed with and eventually displaced other social phenomena and took over their functions. Movies displaced theatrical melodrama, vaudeville and burlesque, just as those had in their turn displaced strolling minstrels, itinerant storytellers and medieval morality plays. The teller of tales functioned not merely as an entertainer, but also as a carrier of information and ideas from community to community. Furthermore, his tales themselves possessed unity, shape and order; they served to explain, order and, so to speak, process the confused flux of experience. They were descriptions of other times and places, illustrations of luck, fate or morality, imaginative journeys of exploration, vehicles for the transmission of ideas. They gave shape and meaning to individual human life and to the totality of human experience simply by having a beginning, a middle, an end, and a point.

In general, then, we can sum up the consequences of such popular story-telling--movies being only the latest technological form it takes--as social control (involving socialization and legitimation), and, somewhat less importantly, cognitive problem solving. Stories never quite replicate the circumstances and situations we face, but that is true of all exemplars. Nevertheless, by the use of imagination they can be applied to real-life problems, giving guidance on such matters as how to cope with the world, what is of true value, what sort of conduct is permissible. In Christianized Europe and America, telling and re-telling the myths, stories and parables of the Bible in the form of lessons, sayings, sermons and morality plays has served these functions. Problem solving by means of imagination (stories) and criticism (better stories) is thought by some philosophers to be the explanation of human progress.

Social pap or an engine of criticism and reflection? These are the poles of the debate this book surveys. The author's position, it will emerge, is a moderate one, somewhere between the extremes.

How does the book relate to social psychology? To some extent this will depend on what social psychology is taken to comprise. If we look at a standard textbook, such as that by Roger Brown (1965) [see Bibliography], we see that the principal concerns of social psychologists are three: the initiation of both children and adults into the rules, obligations

and privileges of social groups (socialization); the effects of
social groups on the development of the individual (personality
formation); and the unique characteristics taken on by people
in groups (collective behavior).[1] There are, as we have already seen, two aspects to movies as a social phenomenon:
their stories or content and their audience or context. Both
content and context may have unintended social consequences.
Parents may raise their children differently, adolescents may
form gangs differently, people may adopt more sophisticated
attitudes towards certain topics, may be more socially at
ease, because of what they have seen in the movies.

Parents can have a brief rest from their children,
children and adolescents can get away from home and be with
each other, people can experience group emotions, above all,
people can establish informal bonds, useful for communication, all on account of having gone to a movie show. So
learning, socialization, personality formation, and even the
way people form into and behave in groups may be influenced
by movie content; while socialization, personality formation
and group behavior are certainly affected by movie context.
It is important to bear both of these aspects of the social
psychology of movies in mind, for much of the standard critical literature focusses exclusively on content. To counter-
act this bias, it is tempting to suggest that the way movie-
going enters into people's lives has more consequences for
socialization, personality formation and group behavior than
does what movies show. Tempting but misleading.

The previous two paragraphs outline matters in a de-
ceptively straightforward way. For not only is there a bias
towards content in the critical literature, there is also a
bias towards social pathology. Much of the literature concerns itself with the extent to which movies may distort
proper socialization of the child, warp personality formation,
cause deviant group behavior. Another task for this volume,
then, will be an attempt to redress the balance by taking
seriously the contrary possibility that movies and movie-
going are interesting as contributions to normal and healthy
socialization, personality formation and group behavior. We
shall also be concerned with very general questions about
movies as social phenomena, looking at the total movie audience and the total movie product. There is the question of
the extent to which movies accurately represent the social
psychology of the societies which they portray and/or the
societies from which they come. There is the much-dis-
cussed question of the effectiveness of movies as tools of

education and propaganda compared to other means of communication. There is the matter of the star, the personality whose impact transcends individual film roles, who becomes the focus of great public interest. And so on.

Those broader matters point to a further theme of some significance: the whole question of the function of movies in society. Some social psychologists would maintain that this question is taken care of by discussing socialization, personality formation and group behavior. I do not accept this. Social significance and psychological significance are different. It seems to me that the same arguments used to establish the independence of social from individual psychology, can also be used to establish the independence of social structures and institutions from psychology. The two basic arguments are very simply stated: the social whole is more than the sum of its human individual parts; and, causal relations can travel down to the individual from the society as well as up from him to the society. The mood of a whole audience, for example, is something more than the sum of the moods of its individual members (parts). Moreover, that mood may change, although the moods of the individual members remain the same. So a group phenomenon like audience mood is not in any simple way a product of the psychology of its members. Similarly, the vagaries of life in Hollywood can be explained as caused by the psychological insecurities of the people who work there; but equally, the structures necessary to create films for a mass market might be said to foster if not cause the psychological insecurities from which its practitioners suffer. We conclude that there are social as well as individual causes.

Allowing, then, that there is an independent social level, we can ask what function movies have at that level. In the literature we find various suggestions: movies are an opiate for the oppressed workers and peasants; they are a replacement for the lost bonds of genuine community; they act as a mirror in which the socially mobile can learn new mores; and so on. While not denying the interest and ingenuity of these and other suggestions, this book will also try to show movies as a force in society, portraying it as it is, as it has been, as it can be, as it should be, as it will be--a critical force sometimes galvanizing a society into action. There are periods in the history of the American cinema when suggesting such a function would have seemed ludicrous; when nothing appeared to be clearer than the dull conventionality of American movies; and if movies were a social force at all they seemed to be a negative, possibly reactionary, even pathological one. Happily, this attitude is no longer unchallenged. Instead, it is widely held that the movies of the last ten years stand in a relationship different from that of their predecessors to the society which produces them. The most talked about (and often most successful) movies of the moment no longer seem to be uniformly conventional, respectable, reassuring.[2] One thinks of Blow-Up (1966), Bonnie and Clyde (1967), The Graduate (1967), Easy Rider (1969), Woodstock (1970), M*A*S*H (1970), Dirty Harry (1971), Carnal Knowledge (1971), The French Connection (1971), A Clockwork Orange (1971), The Last Picture Show (1971), Deliverance (1972), The Godfather (1971), Alice Doesn't Live Here Anymore (1974), Shampoo (1975), One Flew Over the Cuckoo's Nest (1975), Taxi Driver (1976), All the President's Men (1976). Such attitudes as they strike towards society, such values as they display, do not seem consonant with those of the mainstream of American life and values--what is often called Middle America, the silent majority, the established, the straights. Movies like these seem to be countercultural, revolutionary, sometimes nihilistic. This is a startling development. How has the American cinema--once held up as the supreme example of a popular anodyne not to be taken seriously--changed so radically?[3]

While not denying that there has been a change, I sometimes think it is exaggerated. Shifting patterns of moviegoing among the general population, the retirement or death of the oldest generation of filmmakers--who have left behind few successors or replacements--and new technology have forced the movie industry to adapt. But still, we may wonder whether we have been altogether fair in assessing past periods of movies as conventional, dull, not worth taking seriously. If we look again at the movie past, aware of the preconceptions and predilections of earlier writers, we find that the critical posture, the portrayal of society, has long been an important subtradition of the American cinema --buried perhaps for a time, in the forties and fifties, but never completely.

Nevertheless, we seem now to be in a period of real change: at the very least the movie critical of society is no longer buried. At a time when the movies produced are highly diverse it is not surprising, given the subtradition, that some of the most visible and successful movies are well ahead of the thinking of the bulk of the population. Indeed, not only have more critical movies resulted from this diversity, but so also has the constant pushing at the limits of what is tolerable in the depiction of violence and sex, the use of highly intricate and oblique narrative and expositional devices as a matter of course, and other developments to be discussed later on. Matters have come to such a pass that ideas are advocated that are not only far ahead, but so far ahead that the society will never catch up: in particular the sympathetic portrayals of dropping out, iconoclasm and even, in the recent case of Joe, an almost total nihilism (see pages 117-118 below). Yet we are also in a period of unprecedentedly intense self-examination on matters like the generation gap (I Never Sang for My Father, Taking Off, Joe, Where's Poppa, American Graffiti, Harold and Maude, Lords of Flatbush, Harry and Tonto, Next Stop Greenwich Village, Lifeguard) and marriage (see pages 91ff below).

What I shall try to suggest is that our present period of change represents the latest swing of the pendulum, that while critical movies have always been made so have movies which endorse the society more or less as it is. Sometimes critical movies set the tone (the periods 1908-1916, 1930-1934, 1966 to date are examples), at other times they do not (the twenties, the fifties). These swings back and forth must, of course, be part of the general reaction of movie makers to social conditions at the time. They are also governed by internal developments in the film industry (including the rise and fall of individual creators, not to mention intentional actions by government, other industries (e.g., banking, television), religious and other pressure groups, and so on.

* * * * * * *

The plan of the book is this. We begin with a survey of the relevant theoretical questions in social psychology and the literature on them (Chapter I). Then we look at the history of the interaction between movies and society (Chapter II) and try to explain how the present diversified situation has come about (Chapter III). In the final two chapters our concern is the degree to which movies now reflect the reality of society (Chapter IV), and the degree to which they become vehicles of social criticism and protest, oriented to what the reality of society should be (Chapter V).

NOTES

1. Social psychology emerged as a discipline of its

own when it became clear that these sorts of phenomena could not be explained by means of traditional individualistic psychology. The first work in the field was William Mc-Dougall's An Introduction to Social Psychology (1908).

2. For an example of the disquiet they can cause, see Diana Trilling's essay, "Easy Rider and Its Critics" (1970).

3. John Baxter's readable Hollywood in the Sixties totally fails to recognize, never mind confront, this problem.

ACKNOWLEDGMENTS

My thanks to colleagues and students for discussion of the ideas which have found a home in this book, and particularly to Joseph Agassi, Kurt Back, Garth Jowett and Robert Macmillan, all of whom read and commented on the first draft. None of them, of course, can be held responsible for what I say.

I. C. J.

Toronto-London-Hong Kong-Toronto, 1972-1977

THE SOCIAL PSYCHOLOGY OF MOVIES:
HISTORICAL AND THEORETICAL QUESTIONS

> The manners of the youth of
> the country, are in rather
> large degree, made or unmade,
> in the moving picture house.
>
> --Report of the Pennsylvania
> Board of Censors, 1917

Introduction

Appearing from out of nowhere in 1896, movies became within a very short time--say by 1908--the dominant leisure activity of America, especially among the young and the poor. This rapid piece of social change alarmed those who had taken it upon themselves to worry about the moral welfare of society in general and of these classes in particular. Was it a good thing that large numbers of poor young people frequently went into darkened and airless buildings, where the sexes, age groups and social classes mixed freely, there to stare at a flickering screen? Would the cinema environment and what was portrayed there have a good influence or bad upon the audience? If the answer was "bad," the further question arose of whether such bad influences should be controlled. Similar arguments had long surrounded the saloon, cheap literature, theater and vaudeville. The cheapness, mass popularity, visibility and possible influence of the movies pushed them to the center of the discussion. This discussion was to be long drawn out. Until television replaced movies as the major mass medium in the early fifties, the problem of how to control the alleged influence of the movies was constantly being investigated from local level of city censors to that of United States Senate investigating committees.[1]

Many discussions about the social psychology or soci-

ology of movies take their cue from this long-running public
debate and immediately zero in on the problems of censorship and control.   Certainly it was often these practical concerns which stimulated and financed serious study of the influence of the movies.   But scholarly interest in this topic
was legitimate only because underlying the practical problem
lay a theoretical one: do movies influence their audiences?
From this main problem flow others: if movies influence
their audiences how do they do so, and is this influence for
good or ill?   Much the most widespread answer was (and is)
that movies were (and are) an influence--although, as we
shall see, people were (and are) unclear as to how that influence comes about.   Remarkably, in the first three decades
of the century the wrath even of those who most roundly denounced movies was tempered by their conviction that the influence of movies was inherently neither good nor bad.   Much
of what was being shown may have seemed to them bad, but
they also sensed immense potential for good.   Their oppo-
nents were to be found amongst those libertarians who opposed censorship and control because of a basic skepticism
about the movies' capacity to influence at all, whether for
good or ill.   And so emerged the issues which were to be
debated for nearly fifty years.

All this is ancient history.   Today, confronted with
questions about the extent to which movies can influence conduct and values, and whether for good or ill, most scholars
adopt the skeptical posture and ask how "effects" can be
quantified, and what would count as an "adverse" effect and
why.   Such skepticism may be the temper of the times; but
it also may have come about because over the years difficulties have been discovered in the positions of both sides of
the debate.   When the debate began in the early years of this
century, most of those taking part were not skeptical: they
thought they knew what was right and what was wrong, and
they also thought they knew an influence when they say one.
Some were therefore bold enough to accuse the movies of
having adverse effects on people, and especially on "im-
pressionable" children.   Their concern cannot be dismissed
as the product of lurid imagination.   Something was going on
in American society which made them apprehensive and
started the search for causes.   Little did they know, but the
entire social order of the late nineteenth century was being
undermined.   The nation was undergoing a period of very
rapid social change, including changes in outlook and values
that could not but alarm many sober citizens.   The crime
rate was increasing, and at the same time the idea that

criminals were normal people warped by bad influences in the environment was replacing the older idea that criminal tendencies were inborn. Like cheap and sensational popular literature, like vaudeville and like the saloon, movies were highly visible and highly dubious. Their novelty and their unprecedented growth gave credence to speculation that they were a cause rather than an effect of the social upheaval which was underway. Many who harbored suspicions about the movies' power to influence society must have felt their worst fears were confirmed when in 1915 serious race riots followed the showing of The Birth of a Nation in certain abolitionist cities (Cripps 1963, 1977; Carter 1960). And the appearance of tendentious academic and pseudo-academic literature helped such suspicions to grow. The professors were not unanimous, however; Harvard was pitted against Columbia. In 1916, Hugo Munsterberg, a professor of psychology at Harvard, published The Photoplay: A Psychological Study. He did not seem unduly worried about the influence of movies, but stressed their capacity to represent reality and free the consciousness from present space and time. It was not long before a young professor of psychology at Columbia added his academic prestige to the alarmists' case. In 1921 the popular magazine Scientific Monthly published a piece by A. T. Poffenberger entitled "Movies and Crime." Poffenberger was an applied psychologist, very interested in advertising and in taste and smell. His view was that there was an unhealthy connection between movies and crime, and therefore that films were a danger and had to be closely monitored. His status as a prophet of gloom was high, and more moderate voices, such as those of the Rev. J. J. Phelan (Motion Pictures as a Phase of Commercialized Amusement in Toledo, Ohio, 1919), or the critic Tamar Lane (What's Wrong with the Movies?, 1923--answer, not much that a few good movies won't rectify), or the occasional papers delivered to the National Conference on Social Work (1920, 1922, 1927) and such academic works as Child and Society by Phyllis Blanchard (1928), and Children and the Movies by Alice Miller Mitchell (1929), were drowned out by the alarmists, especially when Ellis Oberholtzer, chairman of the Pennsylvania Board of Censors, had denounced The Morals of the Movies in 1922.

We cannot, then, glibly argue that rapid social change bamboozled unsophisticated thinkers into putting the blame on movies and other popular entertainments. At the very least it must be conceded that treating the movies as a causal factor in society was an academically respectable idea, not just

the property of pressure groups and moral reformers. And
is not this reasonable enough? When two striking events are
going on together it is easy to conclude that one is causing
the other, and such a conclusion is very difficult to rebut.
The weight of academic evidence has never, in all these years
of research, told in favor of the alarmists. Yet any research-
er who was prepared to endorse alarmist sentiment was taken
up in a way that non-alarmists were not. We must conclude,
I suppose, that the public--or its newspapers and elected rep-
resentatives--listens to what it wants to hear. The further
question then arises, why is that what they want to hear?
What has the articulate public got against the movies? The
answer--that they need a scapegoat, a distraction to take attention away from other matters--is hackneyed, but perhaps
the best one can do.

So what began as a practical concern that the movies
were a bad influence was very quickly translated to the theoretical level. If movies were an influence, it seemed that
they could exert that influence in a number of ways: by teaching the wrong values (e.g., by showing criminals and others
getting away with their misdeeds); by causing psychological
damage (such as enjoyment of violence or excessive preoccupation with sex); and by provoking undesirable group behavior (strikes, riots, panics, etc.). To teach the wrong values
is to thwart socialization; to cause psychological damage is to
warp the process of personality formation; to provoke panic
and such was not the sort of collective behavior society wanted. Each of these is a key area of social psychology, a subject which seeks explanations of socialization, personality formation and group behavior. These theoretical concerns are
quite distinct from those of psychology and sociology, with
both of which social psychology is sometimes confused, and
to both of which it grants a legitimate place. [2,3] At the
points where society and the individual interact strongly,
social psychology comes into its own. Media--like the mov-
ies--are such points; hence the interest displayed in the media by social psychology. There has been substantial media
research in all three areas of concern, especially insofar as
children are involved.

Out of all the possible topics, three in particular dominate the literature. One, already mentioned, is censorship.
A second is violence. And a third is propaganda. While
all three are perfectly legitimate concerns of a social psychology of the movies, quite disproportionate interest in them
is displayed in the literature. Of the three, propaganda is

perhaps of special interest because it can represent some sort of experimental test of the matter of influence. Movie propagandizing is the attempt to influence socialization, personality formation or group behavior by means of films. Since such a purpose can be known beforehand it is possible to test for its success or lack of it afterwards, by the use of controls. Since governments are interested in making propaganda, especially in wartime, they have made money available for research into this topic (see especially Hovland, Lumsdaine, Sheffield 1949, Fearing 1950, and the survey in Klapper 1961). Where there is money there will be research; where there is research there will be literature. It does not follow that the space devoted to a topic in the literature is in proportion to its intrinsic theoretical importance.

It is for this reason that we shall be wary of the study of propaganda in this volume. For similar reasons, we shall be wary of the two connected topics: violence and censorship. The portrayal of violence on the screen and its impact upon adults and children is like propaganda in that it looks like a clear-cut topic that can be studied empirically. Studies of propaganda and of violence fuse in the study of censorship. If films can be successful propaganda--for a political cause or for sexual liberation, or for violent personal behavior--then they call forth the question of whether and in what ways they should be censored. Since these have become matters of public debate, research money has become available. The result is a vast and sometimes entertaining literature on the history of censorship, Mrs. Grundy-ism, anomalies and inconsistencies in censorship practices, and the moral and legal issues of paternalism and free speech. While all of this may be grist to the mill of academic social psychology, that discipline must nevertheless establish its own priorities.

Literature Survey

All students of the mass media are indebted to Joseph Klapper who in 1961 published an exhaustive survey of the literature under the title, The Effects of Mass Communication. Sooner or later, whoever studies the social psychology of the mass media must work through it. But perhaps in an introductory work such as this, a simpler and quicker survey will set things going. Looking at the literature "politically," as it were, one can isolate three "parties": pessimists, neutrals, and optimists. Methodologically, the literature can be divided into experimentalists and a-priori analysts. This generates six groups which we can diagram as shown in Table 1.

Table 1

EXPERIMENTALISTS	ANALYSTS
PESSIMISTS	
Experimental evidence warrants taking seriously the dangers of movies as weapons of propaganda for political causes, violence, or crime.	Moral argument and/or content analysis of the covert as well as the overt thematics of movies reveals them to be a social, political danger or anodyne.
NEUTRALISTS	
Such evidence as there is tells decisively on neither side.	Such analysis as is possible is difficult if not impossible to interpret.
OPTIMISTS	
Experimental evidence shows that movies do not usurp family or school influence but rather are used by viewers to reinforce views and values already absorbed.	Movies are a great improvement on popular entertainments of yesteryear and seem not only harmless but in some ways beneficial as horizon-widening.

It would be grossly unfair to suggest that any individual author fits neatly into one box only, without overlap or qualification. But, for what it is worth, let us say that the Payne Fund Studies of the early thirties are good examples of careful, experimental and academic neutrality (experimentalist/neutral). Well financed, researched and designed by serious scholars, they detected in the impact of movies on society some dangers, some benefits, but no tilt one way or the other. There is good reason to think that this balanced outcome disappointed the studies' sponsors, because a popularization was commissioned under the title Our Movie Made Children (1933) in which one H. J. Forman attempted to show that the studies reinforced pessimism (this to the consternation of some of the researchers). Forman's book (experimentalist/pessimist) went too far, and drew a withering counterblast from Roman Catholic philosopher Mortimer Adler, who argued in Art and Prudence (1937) that no scientific findings were at all relevant to prudential judgment (analyst/optimist). Amusingly enough, the movie industry itself then commissioned a popularization of Adler's weighty tome under the title Are We Movie Made? (1938) by Raymond Moley (see Jowett 1976).

More recently, we have seen a storm of controversy over the Report of the President's Commission on Obscenity and Pornography (1970) which, after another round of well financed technical studies by academic psychologists and sociologists, concluded that there was cause for neither alarm nor indifference, but perhaps for more sensible laws.

By "analysts" I do not mean only psychoanalysts, but also those who work out their views from first principles rather than from empirical research. Adler did this from his neo-Thomist moral philosophy, but ended up neutral or optimistic; the entire operations of the now-defunct Catholic Legion of Decency turned on the view that there was such a thing as the moral law and that a lot of films did not measure up to it (analyst/pessimist). Recently (1972), in Great Britain, a self-constituted committee on pornography headed by the rather eccentric peer Lord Longford produced an alarmist "report" based on "research." That research was no more than the result of small-group discussions which were then written up by collaborators with pre-formed views (analyst/pessimists). Not only moralists, but also psychoanalysts and psychiatrists argue this way. One can come across dire warnings about Walt Disney films like Bambi and Dumbo because they treat of the themes of loss or even death of the mother--a terrifying thought for a child. A common syllogism among the analysts is this: movies are escape, escape is bad, therefore, movies are bad.

Undoubtedly the most influential of the analysts, however, are the Marxists--or shall we say neo-Marxists, since Marx himself did not pronounce upon the mass media? It is not clear to me why so much writing on the mass media should be by Marxists. There is Arnold Hauser's The Social History of Art (1951), which concludes with a section on movies; there is the work of the culture critics Dwight Macdonald (1954), Richard Hoggart (1957), and Raymond Williams (1958); and there is the German contingent: T. W. Adorno (1941) on

popular music, his student Herta Herzog (and Rudolf Arnheim)
on radio soap opera (1943), and Siegfried Kracauer (1947) on
film. Edward Shils (1957) has drawn attention to the number
of what he calls 'disappointed Marxists' in the study of the
mass media. I would go further than Shils and claim that
the strong association of film studies, both social and aesthetic, with left-radicalism is a curiosity that needs explanation, of which two kinds--ideological and institutional--can
be advanced.

For Marxists, the very existence of the mass media,
as well as their popularity, present ideological problems.
Why are they so characteristic of advanced capitalist societies? Why are they so popular with the masses and the bour-
geoisie, but not with the literati and intellectuals? What
should be the attitude of organized Marxism (e.g., the Communist Party) be to the media? One idea was that the media pur-
veyed popular stories to distract the masses from the miser-
ies of their exploitation. [4] Lenin added a new element when
in 1925 he suggested adding film to the Party's weaponry of
agitation and propaganda. The revolutionaries had long made
use of the printing press and, later, in Russia, the agit-prop
theater (in factories, for example). But film was a truly
mass instrument, easily reproduced and broadcast, and also
able to stir up the masses, to raise their revolutionary consciousness. Well and good, if you happen to live in a communist state. But what of the institutional role of the movies
in the non-communist world? If they are such good tools of
propaganda, to what uses are they being put in the capitalist
world? Here the German context of the discussions becomes
important. For in the same period in which intellectuals were
first coming to grips with movies, the nineteen-twenties, they
were also having to come to terms with very serious economic and political disturbance. The capitalist social order appeared to be in its death spasms with strikes, riots, insur-
rections, galloping inflation, the crash and the Great Depression throwing millions out of work and, emerging from it all,
Hitler and his Nazi party. German intellectuals were fascinated by fascism, by this "new barbarism." Their Marxism
told them it was the last fling of the capitalist social order.
Fascism relied, to an extraordinary extent, on collective rituals like rallies, marches, demonstrations, uniforms, titles
and, significantly, the mass media of radio and the movies.
So while in Russia, Britain, and France, Marxists were able
to believe in the movies--especially Russian movies and realistic documentary movies--the German intellectuals developed
an alternative Marxist view in which movies, like all the mass

media, could be denounced as weapons in the hands of reaction.

Transplanted as a group to the United States, many of these German Marxist intellectuals turned their attention to radio, pop music and, finally, movies. By importing them as a group, America imported their ideology ready-made. And what were the preoccupations of these German intellectuals in the land they had come to to escape fascism? Why, fascism--what else? And especially, warning signs of incipient fascism. The recurring nightmare seems to have been that refuge America--capitalist, economically troubled, media-saturated--might go the way of Germany. Adorno himself wrote some condescending articles about pop music and presided over a study (1950) which argued that there was in America such a thing as an "authoritarian personality," i. e., an identifiable psychological type that would be disposed to accede to or even welcome fascism. In and of itself this theory has had enormous influence, since it brushes aside the classical notion that political choices are made rationally after weighing arguments for and against each alternative. Not only could emotion enter politics, as everyone admitted, but seemingly also the personality structure too. Hence, further, any influence on personality formation, such as movies, that encouraged the formation of the authoritarian personality was to be deplored.

In film studies themselves, the work of Adorno's associate Siegfried Kracauer was also very influential. A newspaper film critic before fleeing Germany, Kracauer attached himself to the Museum of Modern Art Film Library but also, during the war, seems to have worked for the United States government. His theory was this. Fascism is not just a political system, it is a view of life, a kind of personality, even a certain kind of myth and dream symbolism. He maintains that such fascist themes can be detected as an undertow in German films as far back as 1919. That gloom, humiliation, authoritarian figures, Aryan legends, and fantasies about various sexual matters--all indicative of incipient fascism--pervade many key German movies.

Kracauer himself went on to study American films and try to read the tea leaves as to what they portended (1946, 1948). But his style of analysis was taken up by less politically oriented writers including Parker Tyler (1944, 1947), Martha Wolfenstein and Nathan Leites (1950), and Barbara Deming (1969). All of these were more neutral than pes-

Fifties gothic--or, nasty goings-on in the boardroom. The 1954 M.G.M. film of Cameron Hawley's novel Executive Suite seemed to expose cut-throat, corporate politics, yet everything works out for the best. Robert Wise directed a star-studded cast including (L to R): Louis Calhern, Paul Douglas, Frederick March, Barbara Stanwyck, William Holden and Nina Foch.

simistic, but they followed Kracauer in thinking that movies made for the popular audience revealed things about the American consciousness. Kracauer himself went on to look at the way Hollywood stereotypes nationalities. But his heirs in this sort of study were Dorothy Jones (1942, 1945, 1950, 1955), Fred Elkin (1949, 1954, 1955) and David Riesman (1950), the former of whom pioneered "experimental" content analysis, making possible her own studies of war in Hollywood movies, and of the portrayal of China and India, as well as Elkin's studies of the sociological significance of star images, and Riesman's as well as Elkin's analysis of the values of popular films (all neutralist).

By and large the opposition to the pessimistic analysis has come from non-Marxists such as Edward Shils (1957, 1961), Bernard Berelson (1961), Raymond Bauer (1960, 1963), Klapper himself, D. W. Brogan (1954) and W. Stephenson (1967). None of them has written about films as such, only about popular culture in general. They have attacked the condescension and alarmism of the pessimists, arguing that movies and other media are rather harmless pastimes and diversions, no worse than gossip or playing bridge, possibly better than drinking or gambling, certainly better than bear baiting, cock fighting, watching public executions, roaming the streets and other ways of passing the time popular among the masses in bygone days.

Serious empirical research on movies got a big boost from the already mentioned Payne Fund Studies, begun about 1928 and published in 1933. They were designed to investigate whether there was a connection between crime and movies. Studies were made of film content, of children's movie behavior, of children's sleep, of their school performance, and so on, to see if personality, socialization or group behavior was being warped by movies. A line of investigation inspired by their example continues down to our own day. In 1941 (Hollywood: The Movie Colony, the Movie Makers by Leo Rosten) and again in 1950 (Hollywood--The Dream Factory by Hortense Powdermaker) Hollywood itself was studied as a community, sociologist Rosten sceptically neutral, anthropologist Powdermaker full of dire warnings. In Britain in the late forties J. P. Mayer probed the role of films in the psychological lives of British movie fans by means of autobiographies and questionnaires (Sociology of Film, 1946; British Cinemas and Their Audiences, 1948). He was very pessimistic, so much so that when his warnings were not heeded he gave up movie research (1972). In the fifties two crucial pieces of optimistic research were published: first, Elihu Katz and Paul Lazarsfeld in Personal Influence (1955) undermined much of the case of those who worried about media "influence" by showing that there was no direct influence flowing from the screen to the viewer's mind. They argued that influence was "mediated" by other persons, especially the family and friends. There were two steps in the flow of influence. Movie choices and reactions were governed by "taste leaders" who emerged in each clique of friends. Secondly, soon after, Herbert Gans (1961, 1966) tried to explain why American movies and television programs went down so well in Britain, especially with the workers. Katz-Lazarsfeld and Gans could be classed as optimists.

In independent reviews of the evidence about the whole theory of media in mass society R. and A. Bauer (1960) and Harold Wilensky (1964) came to opposite conclusions, the former strongly optimistic, the latter deeply pessimistic.

To conclude this survey I must concentrate once more upon the pessimists. In the fifties the theory that movies cause crime or even delinquency seems to have undergone subtle modification. [5] Now the question was, what effects on people did the portrayal of violence have? The crucial papers are by Albert (1957), Lovaas (1961), Bandura and Ross (1963) and Berkowitz (various dates from 1963 on). The research usually consists of showing adult or child subjects a violent film (boxing or cartoon) and utilizing various devices to detect whether this cathects their aggressions or not. Children are watched to see if they play "aggressive" games or attack Bobo dolls more, subjects are deliberately frustrated or provoked before the screening, sometimes data are produced by allowing annoyed subjects to administer electric shocks to their tormentors. One large claim that is made in behalf of this research is that it has exploded the theory of catharsis. It has not shown long-term or serious increases in aggression among subjects. Such research continues.

Some of these sketches of the literature will be filled out in more detail later. Now, however, we can come back to our basic theoretical questions about movies and their influence.

Do Movies Influence, and If So, How?

Movies obviously do have influence. Bonnie and Clyde

created a vogue for clothes fashioned after those of the thirties. So many women factory workers copied Veronica Lake's
peek-a-boo hairstyle during the Second World War, that governments actively promoted the snood as a means of prevent-
ing such long hair styles getting caught in the machines. Few
historians doubt that films were a factor in the massive mi-
gration to California from all over the United States and Canada that has been going on since World War I. It is more
difficult to decide such question as whether the smart-aleck
behavior by children in American movies and television programs is a cause or an effect of the number of smart-aleck
children there are in reality. However that may be, makers
of propaganda movies, television commercials, educational
and documentary films share this very commonsensical view
that movies can directly influence people. However, in neither the Bonnie and Clyde nor Veronica Lake cases, above,
was the influence intentional.

Once it is asserted that intentional influence, or manipulation, is possible, the student of social psychology will
quickly question the model of the susceptible human being
which underlies the thinking of those who engage in studies
of propaganda, violence and censorship. The model, roughly,
sees man as a target, targets being passive recipients of what
is shot at them, as well as very similar to each other. Similarly, the crude theory of influence views man as an anonymous individual bombarded with items of political, sexual or
violent propaganda (messages) to which he reacts or fails to
react. Like a target, man takes what is thrown at him, and
researchers sometimes don't even talk of expression or re-
action--a person, or, at least, a distinguishable face would
be needed for that--but of stimulated behavior. Attention is
concentrated more on whether children punch a Bobo doll
(Lovaas 1961) after seeing a film than on whether they expressed fear, pleasure, dislike, or indifference to the movie
which was unrolled for them. The viewer is seen as something like a mysterious black box: we observe what goes in
and we observe what comes out. But what happens in between, inside, is going on in a darkness both artificial to
the cinema situation and theoretical because of the little we
understand about the workings of the mind. Black boxes,
like targets, are more or less indistinguishable from each
other. Significantly, experimental psychologists usually refer to the persons undergoing their tests as "Ss" (subjects).
Rarely if ever are they singled out as individuals; usually
only the gross social characteristics (class, education, sex,
age, etc.) of the Ss are specified. This is presumably not

simply to protect the privacy or the anonymity of the individuals, but also because individuality is thought to be irrelevant (a marksman does not blame the target if he fails to score). Herbert Gans, a sociologist, has labeled the sort of model we have been discussing "the hypodermic theory" (Gans 1960). Film messages are looked on as being rather like an injection into an anesthetized or hypnotized patient. A key feature of the hypodermic analogy is that the needle and its operator are manipulating (educating or corrupting) a passive audience. No one, of course, thinks the black-box audience is entirely passive or inert. But it is thought to be passive with regard to input. Messages are cooked up by the movie makers and injected into the audience; the audience does not create or adopt the message it receives.

An absurdity of the model is that it leaves us defenseless. If individuality counts not at all, then we are all corrupt, and no censor or critic can protect us (since they are corrupt too). Yet the target-hypodermic theory is usually allied with the censor and control viewpoint: a privileged few, it is said, can resist manipulation and hence can and should protect the rest. These few are rarely identified.

Once the obvious difficulties of anonymity, similarity and passivity are seen, it immediately becomes possible to suggest a different model that better accords with standard ideas in another area of experimental psychology, the psychology of perception. The audience member or the whole audience may continue to be regarded as a black-box, but it has to be one that seems aware of its surroundings and able to control not only its output but also, to an extent, its inputs. This is how our senses are. It is true that our sense organs are bombarded by information sources beyond their control. But what they make of these, how they interpret them, what they construct out of them, is partly under control. We can fail to see and hear what we wish to ignore; we can fail to notice something significant because we are looking for something else. The drawings which are alternatively a duck or a rabbit, receding or protruding cubes, are illustrations of this that are familiar to all beginners in psychology. Perception, we say, is selective. It is an activity of the brain, which imposes organization, structure, meaning on the seamless flux of experience: it constructs what stimulates it into objects, events, processes.

Here, then, we have an alternative model of man with which to explain the influence of movies on the movie audience.

No longer a passive receptor, the moviegoer is armed with a highly active and selective brain. Not only that, however; for his brain works, sees the world, against a background long predating exposure to film influence. What confronts a film is not just a selective-perception mechanism, perhaps, but something better described as a whole person. That person brings into the cinema with him, as it were, a whole social and psychological cloud of context from within which he observes, learns, thinks, feels and acts. This matrix is what confronts, filters, absorbs, and otherwise deals with the messages coming off the screen. Such a theory leads to the conclusion that any influence a film may exert is at least a joint product of the intentions (and accomplishments) of the filmmaker and the predilections and interests of the moviegoer. If it is further granted that all messages are ambiguous to one or another degree, and must be interpreted, we can see why some conclude that propaganda influence is entirely subject controlled: people see and hear only what they want to see and hear and can reinterpret and twist any countervailing points of view to prevent them "getting through."

Important studies of propaganda were made by Cooper and Jahoda (1947) and Cooper and Dinerman (1951). In the first, the researchers studied reactions to some cartoons satirizing "Mr. Biggott" and were intrigued by the various means people found of evading the message. In the second, they studied how audiences reacted to a conscious piece of anti-fascist propaganda, the film Don't Be a Sucker. This was an Army Signal Corps film that showed an American learning that all prejudices are bad, even those you agree with. Various factors, including the glamorous portrayal of the German, blunted or reversed the intended affect. Closely related was the Wiese and Cole study (1946) of the commercial film Tomorrow the World. This portrayed the destructive effect of a malicious little German boy's coming to a small American town and poisoning people's minds with fascist ideas. Those seeing the film who were already pro-German or easy-going about Nazism did not notice the anti-Nazi message, but thought that on the whole the young boy's behavior was all right--if a bit extreme. He could not, they thought, be blamed for the tragedy that ensued.

Sometimes the propaganda message will not just be missed, it will be reversed; as when anti-Semitic or anti-Negro remarks in a film campaigning against anti-Semitism or color prejudice are absorbed into the viewers' anti-Semitism or color prejudice. Selective perception so strong that

the intended message is reversed has been labeled the "boomerang effect." Put roughly, the boomerang effect is operating
when reactions to a film's "message" can be predicted on the
basis of previously held audience attitudes.

As well as causing reinforcement and boomeranging,
selective perception has caused subjects simply to fail totally
to grasp the message. Wilson (1961) reports from Africa on
the problem of selective perception that results in persons'
not knowing how to look at or "read" films, a phenomenon
he calls "film illiteracy." A health education film was shown
to some African villagers and then they were asked to say
what had interested them in what they had seen. Considerable
interest was expressed in the chicken. The researchers were
not aware there was a chicken in the film at all. Rerunning
the movie they noticed a chicken occasionally scratching about
in the background. Conclusion: taking in what goes on in the
frame of a film is a learned response, like the ability to
"read" a two-dimensional photograph in three dimensions.
People used to watching films focus a little in front of the
screen, in order to take in the total scene; film "illiterates"
scan the picture for interesting details. Hence they miss the
point while noticing the chicken.

Many conventions are involved in watching a movie.
These have to be learned, but we take them so much for
granted we hardly notice them. The Africans wanted to know
where a man was going when he went off screen. Panning
the camera, or moving into close-up were "read" as the land-
scape moving, a person growing bigger, or us (the viewers)
walking closer, etc. The researchers had to simplify their
film conventions until the audience had acquired "film literacy."
It took three to four years.

It should be noticed that selective perception goes on
all the time at a mundane level. Hearing two people describe or reading what two critics have written about a film
upon which they disagree is often like hearing about different
films.

Selective perception probably plays an essential role
in the mind's attempt to order and interpret experience.
This in turn is part and parcel of our attempt to cope with
our environment. But if our selection mechanisms are so
strong that they can distort messages, the possibility arises
of systematic distortion of our information about the environment. This will make it harder for us to cope with that en-

vironment, and might even be dangerous. So let us not be tempted to generalize from the boomerang argument any more than we should be tempted to generalize to the faultiness of all perception because of the existence of optical illusions. In the case of the boomerang effect we have a special problem. Here people holding an opinion, whether about VD or Nazism, are asked to contemplate a countervailing opinion. Common sense tells us that this will set up a tension, partly to be released in vacillation and ambivalence, but probably in the end resolved by choosing either the old opinion or the new one. The latter phenomenon, conversion, is familiar enough. Too familiar, for we expect it invariably to accompany propaganda. In fact more common is reversion to the security of the previous opinion and reinterpretation of the propaganda to fit it. This coping with conflicting opinions is sometimes known as "cognitive dissonance," and there is even supposed to be a "theory of cognitive dissonance," which states that if a subject takes an action (such as joining a group that believes in the end of the world) which turns out to be inconsistent with what happens (the world does not end) a tension is generated which results, not in repudiating the group and its beliefs, but in ad hoc adjustments to the beliefs and active proselytizing for new members (Festinger 1957; Schulman 1965).

One may doubt, with Brown (1965), that this is a theory, or that it explains very much. Yet the desire for consistency, consonance, harmony or balance among one's beliefs, and between one's beliefs and the beliefs of the groups to which we attach ourselves, is very strong. Unless we grasp this the boomerang effect appears to be really quirky.

Clearly the hypodermic theory and the selective perception theory of movie influence are in conflict. One looks to the movie as an influence; the other looks to the person as controlling influence. One sees the person as passively acted upon; the other sees the person as actively controlling. Equally clearly, persons are sometimes converted--do sometimes display the boomerang effect. So we are neither impervious to influence nor helpless before it. Any theory of influence will have to allow for this. The leading candidate is the already mentioned theory of "personal influence" by Katz and Lazarsfeld (1955). This is a rich study which ends up by showing that there is almost no direct influence of message on person. That the message is nearly always mediated by a group or an opinion leader or both. The authors call this "the two-step flow of communications" because their research revealed that ideas flow from the media to the opinion leaders and from them to the less active sections of the population:

> influences from the mass media, are, so to say, refracted by the personal environment of the ultimate consumer. Whether one person influenced another did not depend only upon the relation between the two, but also upon the manner in which they were embedded into circles of friends, relatives or co-workers [pp. 7-8].

These opinion leaders, in turn, admitted to getting a lot out of the movies, and they also were more frequent users of other media, such as radio and magazines. Katz and Lazarsfeld wondered who these opinion leaders were. They eliminated the possibility that they were especially "popular" or that they had high social status. They concluded:

> it is evident that movie-going is a main theme of American youth culture and that the influentials in this realm arise from the ranks of the young and carefree. What's more, within every life-cycle bracket, the leader is the more frequent moviegoer, more particular about what she sees and more exogamous in her choice of companions.
>
> Movie-going, we have seen, is not a solitary activity; people go to the movies in groups. The flow of influence in this realm, we think, takes place largely within these movie-going groups which are usually made up of age peers. But when it comes to consulting a movie 'expert,' people of all ages turn to the girls [p. 308].

Group dynamics, then, buffers or mediates between the media message and the influence on the mass. If the peer group changes its view, this will be because influentials changed their views, and they are exposed to a wide variety of media influences among which they select.

We cannot leave this topic without expanding a little on David Riesman's explanation of what is going on in all this. Riesman argued in The Lonely Crowd (1950) that people's overall outlook, values, beliefs had been, once upon a time, handed down by tradition from generation to generation

In the fifties the corporation success ladder takes its toll.
Here, only the dog bothers to look up when The Man in the
Gray Flannel Suit (Gregory Peck) comes home to the suburbs from a hard day in the Madison Avenue rat race. The
1956 Twentieth Century-Fox film, from Sloan Wilson's novel,
was written and directed by Nunnally Johnson.

("tradition directed"). Our rapidly changing and iconoclastic
society has repudiated tradition--indeed the creation of America itself was such a repudiation. However, for as long as
America was a wilderness frontier, those persons adapted
best who had internalized strong values and beliefs and who
could thus keep going, however bad conditions became, however prolonged their isolation. But this "inner-directed"
type thrived only in the transitional conditions of the frontier
period. Once the frontier was closed, and the rigors of the
environment lessened, conditions favored other personality
types. Nowadays, under urbanization and mass communication, the formative influence is no longer tradition, the type
produced no longer inner directed. Today, the dominant influence is others--family, school, community and above all
the adolescent "jury of their peers". The product of this
socialization process no longer seeks inner sources of direc-

tion. He is "other directed," accepting the values and conduct of those who surround him and to whose company he wishes to "belong." The mass media form the network which links the dispersed peer groups, and the media work through the process of "personal influence."

Other Things Besides Influence

So far, the theories we have looked at have treated films and their audiences as though they were transmitters and receivers respectively. We have seen that transmission is a process fraught with difficulty and that reception is a context-bound process, both the immediate context in a theater and the "invisible" context of the background and education a person carries around with him. All of the theories looked at so far are information orientated: messages are sent out and received, offered and taken. This information is thought to have a bearing on how the individual behaves and hence is an aspect of social control. "Social control" means the ways in which the actions of people are constrained by social institutions and group pressures and by the behavior of other people. This brings us to the work of Stephenson (1967), who has tried to argue that there is another entire dimension to the study of the media of mass communication that has little to do with influence or social control at all. The other dimension is play. "Play is disinterested, self-sufficient, an interlude from work. It brings no material gain" (pp. 192-93). Stephenson thinks that many of us go to the movies simply as play: we select them as a pleasant interlude, and our selections converge in order to give us something to talk about and to make life easier by normalizing manners. Fads, manners, fashions, tastes, are in this category of "convergent selectivity." Stephenson's idea supplements rather than replaces what has been said about social control; anthropologist John Roberts has argued convincingly that games play an important role in the way society works. To be specific, Roberts (1966) sees games of chance as modeling a person's powerlessness in the face of uncertainty, and the learning resulting from playing with these models "may give individuals and groups strength to endure bad times in the hope of brighter futures" (p. 143). Games of strategy, similarly, are expressive of wider themes in the culture and sometimes are a form of self-testing. However all this may be, Stephenson's idea also fits well with our theme that concentration on social control aspects of movies focuses interest on the possible damage the movies can do, or the uplift they can con-

vey, rather than on their integration into the normal life of
the audience, seeking relaxation and enjoyment. The position
could be summed up by saying that while all entertainment
has at least an element of social control, not all social control has an element of entertainment.

One of the ways in which an attempt has been made to
link the play aspects of movie-going with healthy socialization
is found in Brodbeck (1955). He suggests looking at movie-
going as a problem-solving activity for children. A child is
engaged constantly in learning the skills necessary to survive
and thrive in society: to talk, read, count, tell time, grasp
the values, norms and customs of his society, its laws, history and rituals. Psychologically he is trying to picture or
map his environment and to separate out and identify his own
self. He is developing his own ideas, opinions, emotional
reactions and attitudes to other people. The fantasy material
which appears on the movie screen can be regarded as experimental experience without real-life restrictions. Young children take a special interest in violence and sudden death in
movies, adolescents in themes of romantic love. In general,
children pay more attention if the film is new to them, whether Gene Autry or Son of Flubber (further adventures of the
professor who invented "flying rubber"), less attention if it
is familiar. They may be thought to have absorbed what they
can.

Fearing (1947) argues in a similar way that the adult
filmgoer uses the film to help come to terms with the larger
environment: his aims, dispositions and problems in that en-
terprise decisively affect what he gets out of pictures. Fearing goes on to generalize this view in his classic study "Towards a Psychological Theory of Communication" (1953).
He sets out to give a general account of the human need for
communication and its effect on individuals. What he says
applies to movies. Fundamentally, the individual communi-
cates with and to others in his environment in order to structure that environment in such a way that tension brought on
by instabilities and disequilibrium during previous interaction
with the environment is lessened or discharged. This allows
for the view both that movies are a distraction, an escape
valve, and that their content can be useful in learning and
problem solving. [7]

It may sound a trifle absurd to say that the cinema
can be used for learning and problem solving, given that
movies are so full of tricks and distortions. The tendency

is to think immediately of individuals' learning to talk out of the corner of their mouths like Bogart, or to solve all problems with their fists. If the movie audience does learn and problem-solve it must be more critical and selective of what it is exposed to than these examples suggest. Perhaps more in the trivia of everyday--how to dress with taste, to conduct oneself in social situations, to react to crises, and so on--is the movie a medium of education. And insofar as ordinary people grapple with such problems, they can as it were see different movies as alternatives, selected scenarios which can be thought or imagined through as part of the trial-and-error process of reaching a solution.

Good Influence or Bad

It has frequently been argued, especially by social scientists influenced by the Frankfurt Institut für Sozialforschung (its luminaries: Adorno, Gerth, Horkheimer, Kracauer, Mannheim, Marcuse, et al.) that the global function of mass media like movies and radio is to cement together the alienated and atomized ("privatized" might be the current word) industrial workers of the mass society. As we have noted, this view, that capitalism has resulted in a fragmented mass society whose members are no longer held together by the bonds of family, locality, religion, and tradition, seems to have been offered originally as an explanation of the rise of Hitler, and especially his effective use of the mass media. Subsequently, the explanation was generalized, and any advanced mass society heavily penetrated by the media was thought to be in danger of totalitarianism. Movies were a particular target for this kind of attack, as analyses poured forth in the forties detecting totalitarian elements in Hollywood movies, and seeing danger in the importance Hollywood had assumed in American life. Hence, the excessive attention paid to the possibly damaging effects of the movies and to propaganda.

All hope was not lost, however. Bauer and Bauer (1960) show clearly enough that the mass society argument is predicated on a dubious analysis of society and the place of the media in it. For one thing, statistics show that Americans are not more passive, criminal, or mentally ill than comparable societies. But more important is the fact that research such as that of Katz and Lazarsfeld shows that the primary group and the peer group, both characterized by face-to-face relationships, "control" consumption and the use of communications (see Chapter III).

Much of what has been argued so far about the role
of movies in socialization, personality formation and group
behavior applies straightforwardly enough when we turn to
movie-going instead of movie content. Going to a movie is
a highly organized activity--in the social as well as the perceptual sense--involving selection from a range of unknown
quantities, arrangements with other people, timing of meals
and transportation, disciplined behavior such as waiting, queueing in line, sitting quietly for long periods, leaving in an or-
derly manner, etc. People usually go in small groups of two
or more, which interact strongly but which cut themselves off
from other such groups in lines and in the dark. Comments,
if passed at all, are kept low. And yet the audience as a
whole sometimes acts together, not simply upon entering or
leaving, but in groaning when yet another idiot travelogue de-
lays the arrival of the feature, or the film breaks, in laugh-
ing or shrieking in fear together, or in responding to some
loud appropriate comment made in a lull--a word, a whistle,
an audible kiss. Sociologists call such a collection of people
a quasi-group, since it has some group characteristics, like
propinquity, but lacks identity, continuity and true bonds.
Social psychologists study its collective behavior, especially
in extreme cases, for example if someone should shout
"fire!" and panic ensue.

It is interesting to watch people going to movies.
There is the invisible intelligence network by means of which
they decide a film has to be seen. "Everyone" is talking
about it. Or, some person or persons they regard as significant is commending it. Or, they want to see some movie
or other, and from various sources--word of mouth, trailers,
ads, what they have read, even the look on the faces of the
people who are leaving--this looks the most likely to please.
Then the visible things. Standing in line. Each group talks
quietly, not overtly scrutinizing their neighbors, but register-
ing them in the corners of their eyes. Each group mentally
marks off its territory or space in the queue, and tries not
to be too scrunched up between those in front and behind.
Queue jumpers are watched for and eased back, usually with
nothing said. People act a bit self-consciously, yet try not
to appear to be overhearing the neighboring group when a
silence falls, or to let them overhear. There are occasional
jocular though anonymous exchanges between neighboring groups
about the weather, the usher, the inconvenience. Where-to-
look situations are common, because, like plane or train

riders, people standing in line are in exposed positions where encounters are unavoidable but can be "thinned out" (Goffman 1963, p. 139) so that nonrecognition will be possible later on. Commentators got very excited because during the Second World War in England, where disengagement among the unacquainted is a strict rule, those in trains, sheltering from bombs, queueing for movies and so on began to talk to one another--beyond the frozen formalities. The explanation was thought to be that the sense of a shared stress situation, of "all being in it together," and of course the prolongation of such experiences, even all night long, broke down reserve and created a quasi-community intimacy.

This does not happen in the peacetime movie queue. Couples on a date rarely neck in line. Queueing is an interim. The pattern continues. Tickets are bought, torn, and the moviegoers enter and go through the ritual of choosing seats. At this point quite a few look around--especially in small towns--seeking familiar faces. Then darkness. From this point they address less and less attention to each other (their awareness of the groups around them is lower than it was in the line), and more to the screen. Only eating, smoking, necking, and perhaps a visit to the facilities supervenes. However, awareness of the others' reaction to what goes on on the screen now becomes acute. At a comedy, the genuine enjoyment of the rest of the audience can be infectious; so with tension or horror, or with any kind of emotional involvement, it is easy to get caught up and carried along by the rest. Similarly, when a film is failing to grip, the audience becomes noticeably restless and the atmosphere is ripe for the put-down comment that wrecks the movie.

Obviously, no two audiences experience the same movie in precisely the same way. Even if an audience is simply the sum of its individual parts, that sum will almost never be the same; and if we make "audience" a function of its members plus the film they are seeing, the uniqueness of each audience becomes transparent. Beyond this obvious point, however, I want to argue another: that audience reactions to a film do fall into broad bands about which we can generalize. To put it at its simplest, the audience for The Godfather in Hong Kong will differ radically from the audience for the same film in Topeka, Kansas. The audience for the same film when it is revived on 42nd Street, will be different from the audience were it ever shown at the Radio City Music Hall. Less simply, the buzz of talk in Israeli or Hong Kong cinemas as audiences read the subtitles, or comment to each other, is rather different from the sepulchral silence in which films are greeted in other movie theaters elsewhere.

To go any further with this I need a theory, or something like a theory, to make sense of what is happening. I need a theory of collective perception. Collective perception is my label for general audience reaction to a movie. This is not reducible to the sum of individual reactions since, for example, the mood of an audience is not the same as the moods of its several individuals. Clearly, though, collective perception will bear some strong relationship to the perceptions of its members, even insofar as these are explicable by age, class, ethnic origin, education, and so on.

My contention is that at different times and in different places audiences collectively perceive or, if you like, collectively experience movies in quite different ways. For the poor, movies may be a luxurious entertainment or they may be an extension of their neighborhood get-togethers on patio or stoop. They will thus not only behave appropriately, they will experience appropriately as well. Gans has observed similar processes as work among the working-class Bostonians he studied in The Urban Villagers (1962). They are sceptical of all sympathetic portrayals of the police on television, and hoot and ridicule men dominated by women. They are attentive to individualistic tough adventurers who win through by sheer strength. We know that for the poor movies can function as aspiration: they portray people in relative affluence behaving ordinarily, so the thought comes that maybe affluence is available to the ordinary; they portray people acting out their problems individualistically, relatively free of social constraints, so maybe life can be conducted on those terms. A relatively sophisticated middle-class audience might see such films differently: a drama of upward mobility might seem threatening, and confirm their insecurities. Again, they might regard movie-going as an alternative to listening to music, reading, or some other "cultural experience"-- in which case an attitude of quiet attention to the movie may be expected, denoting an attempt to grasp its intentional meaning. One should not naively think of this middle-class reaction as the correct attitude, or frame, in which collectively to perceive movies. The actual intention of most movies after all is no more than to make money...

We tend to take for granted the experience of going to a show, and the standing which it has in the general flow of our experience. But simply going to a movie in another culture should be enough to shake any feeling that it has always been like that, must be like that. Our experience is particular, not general. In other cultures, items like the rough-and-ready seating, lack of carpeting (and hence echo), general noise level, and the amount of socializing that goes on in cinemas in Israel or Italy, to take two Mediterranean examples, is very different from the almost sepulchral hush that is the norm in cinemas in America, Canada or Britain.

It has to be remembered that the first movie houses were converted stores or amusement arcades, with a screen, some chairs, and a booth for the projector. Even the raked floor was not introduced until special buildings were designed and built. Into these inexpensive places wandered the common man, entering for the first time a new social situation, but one where he was surrounded by his peers, a situation not specially structured, not inhibiting. So, talking, commenting, greeting, eating, and a general lack of awe towards movies and their "parlors" was displayed. For this reason, if for no other, in the early years of this century women, especially respectable unescorted women, did not think them suitable places to go.

The search for respectability, then, was an attempt to attract a new class of customer, by upgrading the place of business. Better and more comfortable seating, carpets ("picture palaces" were being referred to by 1914), longer shows, better lighting, raked floors, larger screens, better films (Famous Players in Famous Plays 1912), higher prices, were only half the battle. A more respectful attitude to the place, to movies as an item of experience, needed to be encouraged. Partly the lush surroundings, ushers, and the higher prices seem to have done the trick. Partly also architecture: vaguely grand, vaguely intimidating (suggesting palace or church), sharply dividing foyer (for social chat) from auditorium (darkened for concentrated viewing), echoes of legitimate theater (proscenium arch, lavishly embroidered curtain to raise, intermission), and such oddities as the gigantic illuminated electric organ which would rise from the front of the stage. Partly also these new-style picture palaces were no longer merely neighborhood walk-ins, they were located in expensive, central locations, such as Broadway.

So wholesome and respectable did "motion picture theaters" (strenuous efforts to get rid of names like "the flickers," "the flicks," "the movies," etc. were never very

successful) become, even in slum districts, that the dubious
or risqué content of some films seemed especially outrageous.
Young ladies and indeed whole families would repair to these
theaters once the new attitudes had become set.   But they
could not but be offended by some of the subjects treated in
the films ("white slavery" especially).   This respectable trade
was what the moguls had wanted and aimed to get, hence
their longstanding ambivalence about censorship.

We of the nineteen-seventies are the inheritors.   Except at children's matinees, people are shushed into silence
when the film begins.   We learn to lower our voices when
speaking to companions, to apologize to those already seated
when we pick our way in, to settle down in our seats quickly
and give our full attention to events on the screen.   We choose
a seat and come to regard it as "ours" for the duration of
the show, not to be taken if we go off for candy or micturi-
tion.   To get there we have passed through a series of well-
marked ritual stages, each one guarded, finally to enter a
limbo of soft comfort and darkness where we can yield up
control of our experience to this huge building and its altar,
the screen.   Entering from outside, the first barrier we
passed was the box office, where an offering was extracted--
an effective device to screen the real devotees from among
the frivolous.   Having paid, we begin to see ourselves as
possessing certain rights and privileges, duties and obligations.   We have the right now to see the film in peace and
quiet, we have the obligation to cooperate in other people's
assertion of these same rights.   None should annoy or interfere with another.   Serious business is at hand.   Beyond the
box office is the foyer, guarded by a functionary who takes
and tears the document issued at the box office.   Thus dou-
ble-checked, we can pass through the foyer and its nutritious
distractions and negotiate our way down narrow aisles to
seats.   Often enough the entrance to the auditorium and its
aisles is also guarded by a torch-bearing functionary, who
demands to see the stub, and then helps in seat selection.

Finally we are in place.   Onto the screen itself
there then come various delaying, working-up and anticipatory material, like the lower half of a music hall bill, the
appetizers at a meal, or the introit at a service.   Adver-
tisements, coming attractions, shorts, and then the titles of
the main offering itself all serve to soften us up for the main
bout.

Clearly, no two sets of people will be in exactly the

same collective frame of mind after all these rites. But reaction can, as I said, be classified into broad bands. At one
extreme there is the collective perception of serious attention.
At the opposite extreme is intermittent attention. Between
them is the middle way or relaxed attention. Serious attention might be described as that given a movie being experienced by a group which has come there to that place at that
time to see that movie and no other. This audience relates
to each other via the movie; that is why they are all there
together--not for example because they all live in the same
neighborhood. Their collective perception will be concentrated
rather in the way individual attention is concentrated on a
carefully selected book.

Relaxed attention will vary a great deal. The group
might be there because they felt like going to a movie, or
because someone they knew was going. Their sense of anticipation is much less, their tension level is lower, they do
not take the whole business seriously, and so on; but they
are ready to settle down into it if it really has something to
offer. They are a bit like people who have casually picked
up a book or a magazine and are flicking through it deciding
whether to read it.

Intermittent attention is the condition so often observed
among television viewers. They are only doing it because
there is nothing much else they feel like doing, or because
they can combine it with other things; there is little possibility of positive response. If someone calls for quiet this
may be treated as ridiculous or annoying. In some curious
way audience interaction with the movie and with each other
can be very intense in conditions of intermittent attention.
Awareness of themselves as members of an audience is sharper, and comments, guffaws and what not, seem in place. The
group is as interested in itself as in the movie.

So we have the two extremes: serious attention,
where the group is barely aware of itself, and is a group
formed solely to have the collective experience; and intermittent attention, where pre-existing groups or quasi-groups
(families, gangs, cliques of friends, people of the same
neighborhood) may come to confront the experience. Relaxed
attention covers the ground between. When and how a movie
is influential must be studied in light of these matters. To
generalize a bit: highbrows nearly always view highbrow
movies, serious people nearly always view serious movies
in a collective condition of serious attention. They may thus

be more influenced by the movie. One great hole in the case
of those who want to censor and control the movies is that
the vast bulk of the audience is usually in a state of relaxed
or intermittent attention.

After the show the film audience disperses, but its
members still share the bond of those who have seen that
film and have responded to it--like some, and unlike others,
depending on whether the audience as a whole showed serious,
relaxed or intermittent attention. A shared taste in films is
a good way to explore a budding friendship. A shared experience of certain films is a form of shared education. That
movie-going has now become so very largely the province
of those under forty is significant in this respect. The sorts
of movies that are being seen now, the sorts of shared experience they constitute, are peculiarly well-suited to those who
are adult, but young; exploratory, not fixed in their outlook
or attachments. Hence, the iconoclasm and irreverence of
many contemporary movies can be tolerated, either because
the audience sympathizes, or because to see them on film
is a harmless way to experiment with shocking ideas. The
movies which draw in the older generation do not at all do
the same thing. They reassure rather than disturb or shock,
and they do this by portraying a stable world with stable values. The Sound of Music, Love Story, The Longest Day, do
not challenge anything. The first tells us that music gives
courage to overcome adversity; the second that love survives
death; the third that leadership and guts win the most crucial
battles. If the coexistence of both kinds of movie shows anything, it shows that since they have both found audiences
there must be at least two kinds of audience. No simplistic
correlation of movies and audience is possible when we remember the discussion earlier. But there has always been
a split between youth and the rest. Adolescents in the process of exploring and trying out the fringes of adulthood are
going to learn and problem-solve from rather different films
and stars than their elders. The very old may be particularly fond of reseeing pictures they enjoyed in their youth.
In arguing this way I am drawing on the ideas of Gans, first
essayed in a very interesting paper (1966) on why, in general,
American movies were so popular in Britain. He found that
the themes, ethos and problems of American films filled a
gap. British films tended to have a middle-class, metropol-
itan orientation and were rarely other than condescending to
the "lower orders." American films, by contrast, frequently
were classless, individualistic, and concerned with the problems of ambition and success. These themes, Gans argued,

were peculiarly appealing to those aspiring to upward social
mobility.

In later works, Gans has gone on to generalize and
suggest that different films will appeal to the many diverse
subcultures of the society, whether they are distinguished
by age, sex, class, ethnic background, or whatever. Given
that television has taken over the job of providing the lowest
common denominator of entertainment for all subcultures, he
looks to the possibility of increasingly diverse programming
of all the mass media to cater for these different subcultures.

Whether one accepts these ideas or not, they are well
worth discussion. It is very difficult to go any further on
the subject of popularity. I have myself proposed (1970, pp.
188-94) what might be called a "snowball" theory. This is
to the effect that a film by some mysterious means or other
gets a clear and positively attractive image in the minds of
certain opinion leaders, and that by word of mouth this snow-
balls. Successful producers, directors and stars can all
point to inexplicable flops, despite lavish publicity; and Hollywood knows very well the phenomenon of the "sleeper," the
film that no one expects much of, but which, without publicity,
becomes a smash hit. Recent sleepers have included M. A. S. H.
(gruesome Korean War medical comedy), The Night of the
Living Dead (the bodies rise from the graveyard one night
and begin killing and eating people), and a host of Italian
"spaghetti" westerns and epics. There appears to be no formula for success: sometimes a follow-up to a picture will
do as well or better; examples are the bikini beach series,
the James Bond series, the Planet of the Apes (apes, not
men, as the superior creature) series, and so on. Other
times the follow-up will flop. But whereas once Hollywood
rarely made a film that didn't turn a profit, the ratio of
unprofitable to profitable films is now higher than it ever
has been (Howe 1965, 1972). To this extent one must go
along with Gans and explain it partly by changes in the audience, but also changes in films. The Sound of Music (pretty
singing) and Love Story (doomed romance) may have been
very popular, but so were The Graduate (the straight world
is a bore), M. A. S. H. (in a mad set-up, only the rebels are
responsible persons) and Bonnie and Clyde (criminals are
beautiful people). How are we to account for this? Surely,
if you loved Sound of Music (sweetness and light) you won't
also have loved (or even have seen) M. A. S. H. (send-up and
gore)? Further than this, though: when Hollywood was en-
joying its time of universal profitability, films like M. A. S. H.

would never have been made. Something has changed in the way films reflect or do not reflect the society. Degrees of violence, iconoclasm and sexual explicitness are nowadays permitted which would have been unimaginable only ten years ago. This certainly is connected with important changes in the texture of the wider society, and not with factors internal to Hollywood. However, what concerns us here is that these films are popular. One reason they would not have been made at an earlier date is that they most probably would not have been popular even if they ever got shown. This may have to do with the fact that the audience for movies in the first two decades of the century, which was young and poor, was overshadowed in the twenties, thirties, and forties by an older, middle-class audience demanding a middle-class outlook. Certainly, a lot of early comedy was iconoclastic (cf. Durgnat 1969). Wholehearted attacks on American society have come and gone and have only recently become a subject for popular art once again. They are not universally approved of, even now. At this point, however, I simply want to reiterate that for the first time one can now see films being made for the popular audience which are way ahead of most of the society, and in some cases way ahead of the whole society. This is the significance of the title of the present book, Movies as Social Criticism.

Episodes and ideas are permitted by censors to be shown in films that ten years ago would have not been tolerated (e.g., the oral sex in Carrie). Is this because such things have become widespread in the society; or the suggestion of such things has become widespread and acceptable in the society; or, do the films as it were lead the society rather than reflect it? There is evidence that America is going through an almost unprecedented period of change in which many of her most fundamental institutions, traditions, and values are being critically reevaluated. Film is peculiarly the medium of those under 25 and might be thought to be one of the vehicles of this critical reevaluation. It is in this sense that films are becoming a medium of social criticism. Some of the most lively and critical intellects in America and in other countries (e.g., Godard) find their natural home in movies. Movies are the medium they were raised on and for which they feel a peculiar love and with which they have a peculiar intimacy. Movies also happen to be the medium preferred by that same generation not only as a creative outlet but also as "passive"[8] entertainment. Thus, both the filmmaker and the film audience are in the slot that might lead to great social change. And film may be the medium that is involved.

Learning from Movies

As we have seen, someone exposed to movies for the first time is not able to see them in the way that those of us who are experienced are able to see them. The capacity to read into a two-dimensional flickering image three-dimensional scenes, to grasp that the frame is not a wall behind which the rest of the scene is hidden, to understand and assimilate shifts of the viewpoint of the camera and the result of cuts, all these are acquired or learned capacities. The process begins in the very small infant who must learn to isolate from the flow of experience that comes in through his eyes and other senses the objects which we customarily think of ourselves as living among. This process is socially controlled, for evidence from the sensory organs of other animals shows us that the flow of experience can be chopped up in ways quite different from that chopped up by our ears, eyes, nose, mouth and feeling extremities. Indeed, there are limits on what we can see and hear, although they are not absolute limits since they vary from person to person. There are other creatures which have quite different limits. Dogs can hear sounds higher than we can detect; bats navigate by echolocation. What we have to learn in the course of growing up is to perceive the world, that is, to "see" in the flow of experience the same sorts of objects that our fellow human beings "see". We have to construct the world in such a way that it is a shared or common world about which we can communicate and to which we can adapt.

Among the first movies that children are exposed to are the cartoons on Saturday morning television and the early part of childrens' cinema performances. In these cartoons the drawing is extremely simplified and the characters are usually not people but animals. However, they are animals with human characteristics. These animals and the cartoons about them are introductions to the movie world and also introductions to the real world of human beings and their relationships. The general features of these anthropomorphic animals are simplified in a way that is not true of the world. In the world of the cartoon animals there is no sexual motivation, there is no serious illness, there is no death (one persistent joke is that animals wreak mayhem on each other without apparent lasting injury), there are none of the tensions that exist between humans because of all of these things. It is also notable that the animals are usually detached from any social world. They are very rarely animals which have a mother or father around, the relationships they have are usually those of buddies or nephew to uncle or brother to brother and this too simplifies the emotional world in which the stories take place. The purpose of all this stylization is to allow very simple and basic story lines with little of the tension and lack of shape or resolution which are to be found in real life or even in more sophisticated stories for adults. This might be seen as a means of introducing children to the larger world. But perhaps a very unsatisfactory means. The real problems with which a typical child is coping at the age when he watches a lot of cartoons include those of coming to terms with a new baby in the family, of developing a sense of self, of resolving tensions with the parents, making friends, coping with the elaborate processes of education in school, grasping the significance of authority figures like teachers and policemen, and very few of these are reflected in any helpful way in the rather mindless cartoons which fill the child's world. One thinks especially of Sylvester endlessly stalking Tweetie Pie and being thwarted by Granny or Butch; of the Road Runner series; of Heckle and Jeckel. On reading over this passage, though, I am persuaded that it is too sweeping. Disney cartoons of Mickey Mouse, Donald Duck, Pluto, Goofy, the Silly Symphonies and so on, are much richer in themes than the three examples above. Tom and Jerry cartoons are often inventive, as are Bugs Bunny, although ambush and mayhem are depressingly frequent. Deputy Dawg is sometimes fun, as are Bullwinkle, Shazam, Forgetful Frank, and some of the futuristic "pupetoons," which are, incidentally, inventive. Despite all this, I still think the cartoon world is hardly even a simulacrum of the world the child inhabits, and hence is not much of a preparation for it. In fairness, one should add that the repetitive simplicity and even brutality of so many of the chase cartoons has to do with devising incidents simple enough to be understood by infants.

Many of the serial movies of past times were similar to these cartoons. Many series on television aimed specifically at children resemble these cartoons and in particular Batman and The Man from U. N. C. L. E. , where crime and mayhem are simplified and have the sting removed from them.

As children grow older, somewhat more complication is allowed to enter into stories for them. Little Women or Pollyanna, and so on, begin to initiate the child into a new world of conflicts. Cats or coyotes stalking birds may release tension, but they do not deal directly with the conflicts the child experiences with other children or with adults, or even the observed conflicts between adults. One frequently sees movies in which the parents are separated, or quarreling, or even divorced, and the children are instrumental in reconciliation. The variation on this is where one parent has been lost by death and the children match up the parent with a suitable mate. The significance of this kind of theme is somewhat different. Here the child's genuine concern to live in a complete family without any parts missing is given concrete shape in the form of dissatisfaction with the lack of a parent, and the story resolves the issue by the ideal solution.

Between the cartoons for children, and the films for adults, there is an intermediate category: the movie which is designed for the family and contains layered meanings to please both children and adults. The Disney Company has long done films like this, and they were followed by the Bullwinkle and Charlie Brown cartoons. To contain material for two or more different levels of sophistication is not easily managed. Perhaps this is why Mary Poppins (a nanny with magic powers) and Bedknobs and Broomsticks (an amateur witch defeats the Germans) are family movies with little to offer those more sophisticated than children.

In many films made for children--and indeed for adults--the stories tend to center around characters that could be classified as heroes (or heroines) and villains. The dramatic logic of this is that a story without heroes or villains is a subtle and complex exercise. A basic premise of much narrative is conflict. Conflict between good and bad is the simplest form of conflict, the most direct and easy to grasp and also the most satisfying when resolved in the proper way. So we could see the use of heroes and villains as a means of illustrating and teaching values. Children and adults are encouraged to identify with the hero, adopt his values and outlook and then to live through the action the hero undertakes in the conflict situation in which he finds himself, and to share in his sense of satisfaction at the way they are resolved.

Mostly, the story of life is not written in terms of heroes and villains, blacks and whites, but rather in various hard-to-distinguish shades of gray. Also, the story of life as we live it rarely has any overall shape to it; still less are its episodes shaped by the satisfactory solution of problems. A further distortion we have yet to touch on is the imposition, for the younger age groups at least, of a happy ending. This may or may not lead the child to expect that conflicts of a similar kind which he encounters in adult life will be similarly resolved happily. It may be a source of fustration (if the growing-up process is in any way inhibited) when a child finds that in the real world conflicts are sometimes resolved for the worse rather than the better, and, more frequently, are not resolved at all. Life, children discover, is not chopped up into neat little stories with a conflict, a beginning, a middle and a nicely-resolved end, but consists rather of a series of overlapping and agonizingly irresolvable conflicts. In stories with a happy ending a reward is provided to those who have acted correctly or virtuously. The notion that correct or decent or virtuous conduct will not necessarily be rewarded but that it should be pursued nevertheless is a somewhat sophisticated idea to which children are not early exposed in the movies.

Up to this point in the argument about whether movies are a good influence or a bad one I have moved fairly freely between films and television. This is to some extent because television has taken over part of the role in the life of the child that was once (say between 1908 and 1950) played by the movies. So far as their effects on socialization, that is, teaching about social life, are concerned, they can be discussed together part of the time. But once we turn our attention from children to their influence on adolescents and adults they can no longer be dealt with together. Let us now draw a contrast between the social psychology of movies and that of television. In addition to the obvious fact that movies are an occasion whereas television is a more or less continuous flow or background, there is also the fact that movies are designed to be seen in the concentration of darkness, among a group assembled for a short time, whereas television is designed to be viewed in the intimate and rather casual surroundings of home, possibly with interruptions, certainly with a few others present, and at all kinds of times. If we look at movies and television not simply as sources of information but also as means of entertainment, we might see that the one cannot easily be substituted for the other. The greater drama and tension involved in organizing oneself to go to a movie show is bound to make the experience a somewhat different one than that which comes from a fairly casual turning of the knob, with little forethought or organization involved, and no expenditure. The popularity on television of half-hour series, of puppet shows, of magazine-type shows with masters of ceremonies, and of cartoons indicates some of the differences. (Television audiences give intermittent attention, rarely relaxed or serious attention). We should guard against the view that movie-watching and television-watching are identical occasions. The literature is full of stories of little groups of children sitting around glassy-eyed on Saturday mornings watching hours of cartoons. Field research on this tends to show that the children interact as much with each other as they do with the television set, provided there is more than one child present. Very often the children will be distracted for long periods while they improvise games, make comments and indulge in horseplay. Thus, we must not assume that television any more than the movies is a total socializing or educational influence. Indeed, such studies of these matters as have been made show that the primary socializing and educational forces are, in order of influence, first, the immediate family; second, the group of friends or relatives with which the child habitually associates; third, the school if the child is going to school, or possibly the media and the story books and comic books if the child is either preschool or peculiarly susceptible to those sources (Maccoby 1964, Danziger 1971). This in itself might not provide much comfort except when it is realized that the first two are regarded as overwhelming sources of information and values whereas the third--even school--is regarded as a marginal source. The only qualification here is that insofar as the school functions as a peer group of significant others, it can loom large in the conveying of information and in the teaching of values. The simplified notion that children slavishly watch and are influenced by and hence imitate what they see on television is no closer to the truth than the old notion that adolescents and even adults were heavily influenced to their detriment by movies. All the evidence is that long before children can "read" movies--in the sense explained at the beginning--they have absorbed a framework of information and values into which the movie is slotted. That is to say the perception and interpretation of the movie is done within a predeveloped mental set, against which the movie's information and ideas are evaluated.

Movies are perhaps more a medium for adolescents than they are for either children or adults. This was not always so, and how it came to be so in relatively recent years will be explained in a later chapter. The bulk of the movie audience is now in the teenage and early twenties age group. This is a particularly significant fact, since adolescence is a time of rapid development and change, highly susceptible to all kinds of influences. The fact that the principal medium to which both children and adults are exposed is television, whereas the principal medium to which adolescents expose themselves is movies, makes us want to look closely at the adolescent interaction with movies to see what sorts of cause-and-effect relations can possibly be guessed at.

I do not treat rock music as a medium because information and socialization are there presented in a highly sophisticated way. But a good deal of what I will say about this fact of adolescents' coming together to be a movie audience and the effect this has upon them would apply to their coming together to be a rock-and-roll audience, whether in a lump as in a rock concert, or as a dispersed small-group audience listening to their record players or having a party with the music playing.

The primary influence on adolescent socialization and education is significantly different from that on the child's. In the teenage years, the primary influences are other adolescents, the peer group. The nuclear family of father, mother, brothers and sisters, recedes into the background, and school, despite valiant struggles no doubt, tends to be evaluated in terms set by the peer group. What the peer group endorses and approves of is likely to be what the adolescent him- or herself endorses and approves of. The development of a sense of self and of identity is achieved mainly in interactions within the peer group and what the peer group itself takes for its ideals of identity. It is a significant fact that the peer group selects from among television, radio and movies, the movies as its primary cohesive medium. Adolescents are mainly interested in each other. They are near enough to adulthood to be able to absorb the kind of information they need to organize their life in the world without much effort. They need to accumulate more information, but this is a continuous process. Their main concern is exploration of each other and of themselves through each other. Strong friendships are made in adolescence; and it can be argued that the attempt to come to terms with emotions which are relatively unrestrained in a child, and especially emotions about themselves and towards each other, has been greatly simplified and advanced by the gradual acceptance of the concept of romantic love. This becomes a standard against which to measure both previous and future relationships with the opposite sex, and hence to cope with them.

Apart from rock music, the adolescent peer group as it were decrees that _their_ medium shall be the movies. The movies have the advantage of being removed from the home; of being preselecting in that not just any old group of people will be at any particular movie, but very likely other adolescents who have heard that the movie is one that adolescents will enjoy; the movies are freer than a hidebound, home-centered, middle-class medium like television to explore the extremities of human experience, and they are hence more interesting to adolescents who are still, after all, exploring the possibilities and limits of experience; and, finally, movies are short. Between two and three hours is all that is spent at the movies, and this leaves a great deal of time for those interactions among the peer group in which I claim adolescents are primarily interested. The focus of adolescent conversation is largely on each other and on shared interests, which are what to some extent bind them to each other. One of the primary shared interests they have is the movies that they have seen or intend to see. These movies are very unlikely to have been seen by their parents and almost certainly unlikely to have been seen by younger children. Hence, the information and experience available to the closed group of the adolescents--if not exclusively, then by and large--are vivid and experimental pieces of information, providing plenty of material for discussion. Just as adolescents will relate to each other partly in terms of who else they know, who else they love, who else they are friends with, they will also relate to each other partly in terms of which films they have seen, which films they like, which films they dislike, which actors and actresses they like or dislike, and so on.

The drift of our argument is to suggest that movies are not, as is so often claimed, a form of escape. They are not like a drug trip in which the subject goes into a trance entirely private to himself, and experiences a sense of being transported from the present world to some different and possibly better or more enjoyable world. This identification-escape theory is a somewhat simple-minded way to interpret what happens in the movie experience. Adolescents are far more interested in exploring and testing each other out than they are in escaping. They escape in the sense that they go to the cinema rather than stay at home. Very often what they would go to the cinema to do is for example to see whether they can stand a horror film, whether they can stay awake for an all-night session at a drive-in, whether they can "dig" a new and exciting experience at the cinema. Those producers who have assumed that because the movie audience is primarily adolescent it should be fed primarily movies about adolescents have made a grave mistake. While it is

true that certain movies about adolescents or young people
and their explorations have been extremely popular, imita-
tions have not been. This is because an endless diet of
movies about other adolescents is not particularly helpful to
the testing and exploring adolescent. Here identification seems
to play a certain part. My suggestion is that the popularity
of The Graduate or Easy Rider had more to do with the portrayal of what were felt to be admirable standards of cool or
of life style rather than with the particular help these films
may have been to adolescents struggling to cope. Benjamin,
the bored, well-off graduate seduced by an older woman,
tearing his girl friend away from the altar, is not a practical example. Neither are the spaced-out motorcyclist drug
peddlers of Easy Rider, cruising through the Southwest. And
indeed stars like Robert Redford or Elliott Gould or Dustin
Hoffman seem to be admired because of a certain style they
adopt both in their films and in life. Bonnie and Clyde on
the other hand, I would maintain, was popular not necessarily
because of any identification, but because the movie appeared
at a time when rebellion and the knocking of sacred cows--par-
ticularly middle-class values--including the sacred cow that
villains were always unglamorous, was coming to the surface.
So it is Warren Beatty and Faye Dunaway who rob banks,
shoot it out with cops, and, finally, make it with each other,
before a beautiful and stylized death.

Adolescents, then, use the cinema (and are used by
the cinema) in ways quite different from children. Adolescents are of course more self-conscious and critical and
selective about what they see, but it should be remembered
that the perspective of their peer group is the crucial deter-
mining factor. It is acceptance in the peer group that the
adolescent seeks, and one of his means is acceptance of peer
group-approved movies. Hence movies for adolescents are
means of group formation and of identity reinforcement; far
less are they sources of information or of values.

So, while I have entered some criticisms of the way
movies introduce children to the social world, I would not
do the same for adolescent movie attendance. Movies are
no more than a part of the entire adolescent subculture.
Elsewhere (1972) I have argued that this subculture has its
heartening as well as its disheartening sides, and that glib
judgments are to be avoided. Having said so much about
adolescents, the next logical step would be to consider whether movies are good influence or a bad influence on adults.
To the extent that they are imaginative, interesting, or cri-

tical I think that they are good; to the extent that they are
unimaginative, dull, or uncritical I think that they are bad.
Trying to gauge these extents is what takes up much of the
rest of this book.

NOTES

1. It surprises me, at least, that there was relatively
little active discussion of another cheap, popular and dubious
leisure activity: professional sport. The morality of playing
for money, the underwriting of violence (boxing, wrestling,
football, hockey), the vicious exploitation of some athletes
by rich owners who make huge profits while trading their
players like horses, strike one as pretty discouraging. Yet
even today such matters will not rouse politicians to vote-
getting wrath, or academics to investigation. However, the
eclipse of professional boxing is very interesting.

2. Both sociology and psychology, it deserves to be
noticed, have adherents with imperialistic tendencies who seek
to deny any legitimate place in ultimate explanations to the
other. "Sociologism" names the position that the only legitimate explanatory social science is sociology, "psychologism"
names the position that the only legitimate explanatory social
science is psychology. Marx is noted for a third imperialism:
"economism."

3. Note 2 is somewhat ahistorical. McDougall, the
founder--if there is one--of social psychology, conceived of
social psychology as an imperialistic extension of psychology
to the social level, the main purpose of which was to reduce
social phenomena to the behavior of individuals. Traces of
this psychological reductionism can be found even in Roger
Brown's Social Psychology (1965) where the reality of social
class is explained away, although McDougall is scarcely mentioned in the book. However that may be, we shall try in
this volume to adopt the nonimperialistic or nonreductionist
concept of social psychology given in the text.

4. This is perhaps to underrate their misery. Truly
exploited and miserable people usually cannot be distracted
by anything, still less by something they must pay for.

5. "Movies cause crime" had simply turned out to
be false. Movie-going has been found not correlated with
crime rates; in fact no evidence of its alleged causal effect

could be found.   The subtle modification was an attempt to rescue the pessimist position.

6.   Unless, of course, the distortion is so systematic that we can make systematic corrections to take account of it--something like what happens when after several days of wearing prismatic spectacles which turn the world upside down, we begin to see things the right way up.   But to correct in this way we have to "know" there is distortion as well as that it is systematic.

7.   Much of this was presaged in the studies of radio soap opera by Herzog (1941, 1944), Arnheim (1944) and Warner and Henry (1948).

8.   As will now be clear, I have many reservations about the notion that film viewing is passive.   But in the sense that making films is more active than viewing them, I use it here.

II

THE MOVIES' CHANGING
RELATIONSHIP TO SOCIETY

Having argued that movies do not, in any simple way, influence children and adolescents so far as their core behavior and values go, but that in complex, context-bound ways they do[1]; having argued also that for these age groups moviegoing as a social institution may be even more important than movie content; and having suggested that movies are more interesting as contributions to the normal growing-up process than they are as causal factors in delinquency and deviance; I have prepared the ground for the bulk of this book, which will focus on movies made for and seen by adults. This is a vast area and includes the study of movies to educate and instruct, the effects of propaganda, the influence of the portrayal of violence or of explicit sex, and so on. Some of these matters will be alluded to occasionally, but I intend to restrict myself to one part of this whole area, namely, the way movies influence people's way of seeing their own society, and the degree to which they are a progressive force-- that is, an encouragement to critical and reflective attitudes toward society and its problems. I do not wish this discussion to be thought on account of the word "progressive" to have any left-wing overtones. Both left and right in politics can be critical of society and look to improve it. So a film does not have to be of the left to be critical or progressive.

To begin with, in this chapter, our concern will be with the most general discussion of the way movies portray society, whether they idealize it, reflect it accurately, fantasize about it, or are critical of it. We shall concentrate exclusively on the American feature entertainment film. An admirable attempt at doing something of the sort for Britain and British films has already been made by Durgnat in A Mirror for England (1970). The only previous study of the American cinema on anything like these lines is by the psychologists Martha Wolfenstein and Nathan Leites in their Movies: A Psychological Study (1950). This landmark had the misfortune to be published just as interest in, and money for, media studies were switching over to television. So the book was in fact out of print for nearly twenty years until its paperback reprint in 1970. It thus regrettably failed to found an ongoing discussion of the issues it raised.

The standard line taken by highbrow and left-wing movie critics has always been that American movies show very little if anything of the truth about America. People are falsified; society is falsified. Why? Movies are a form of escape, so their distortions and glamorizing can be explained as attempts to gratify the audience's fantasies. With this view, if movies are to be taken seriously at all, the symbolism and unconscious significance of these fantasies need to be analyzed. The parallel with the psychoanalytic interpretation of dreams is very obvious, and clearly lay behind the work done along these lines. Just as dreams tell us in symbolic form about the unconscious conflicts with which a person is struggling, and even point the way to solutions of them, so too can the fantasy or dream world of movies be held to signify the deep conflicts going on in society, and also perhaps to point towards solutions. At this level there is a great deal of writing, of which I would single out that of Parker Tyler and Barbara Deming as of most interest.

A lot of this writing is fascinating, as are psychoanalyses of Hamlet or Leonardo. The obvious problem is that an analyst with a patient can test his interpretations by putting them to the dreamer. When movies are read as dreams, there is no interaction between analyst and patient, no check on speculation, and, consequently, a danger of arbitrariness. This is entirely aside from the fact that movies are a group product and, in the case of Hollywood, a politically and culturally somewhat insular group at that. How can the "dreams" of this group tell us about the "dreams" of the much larger group, the audience? The answer is that this film dream world is popular, i.e., it appeals at some deep level of the mind. Thus, what is left out becomes as significant as what is included; the placing of emphasis is as significant as what is included; recurring themes and unselfconscious preoccupations reveal unconscious thoughts, wishes and tensions.

Siegfried Kracauer, for example, a refugee German journalist, set out to show in his From Caligari to Hitler (1947) how certain features of the German national psyche were reflected in German films of the twenties and thirties. The themes of gloom, humiliation, mysticism, authoritarian-

ism and nationalism which portended the rise of the Nazis
were all present in the films of the period for those who could
see, he argued. It amounted to a bold, even reckless hypothesis: look closely at the content of popular art and you may
see the deep forces at work in the national psyche and thus
be able to take precautions if the signs are ominous. Kracauer was a trifle vague about the connection between the popularity of the films and what they revealed about the nation's
psychic life. He moved easily between the esoteric Cabinet
of Dr. Caligari and popular comedies. There is after all no
necessary connection between the conscious enjoyment of films
and their unconscious significance. Quite possibly, films
touching an unconscious nerve would be unpopular.

Kracauer was a major influence on American thinking
about films in the forties and one finds a great many authors
looking at American films the way he had looked at German
films, seeking portents and concluding that fascist traits were
present in the American national psyche. Some of this was
done by or under the influence of refugees so badly frightened
by their own experiences with fascism that they tended to see
it everywhere. Less understandable is why it was so readily
swallowed by American intellectuals (e.g., Powdermaker
1950). As we know, these gloomy portents turned out to be
unfounded. To their credit, Wolfenstein and Leites concentrated their attention on other matters, especially male-fe-
male relationships and that curious figure the "good-bad girl"
(she seems to be bad, but underneath she is good). Since
the period of their analyses (1946-1948) little work has been
done on the portrayal of society on the American screen. In
this chapter we will try to reopen the whole matter, beginning
with an attempt to identify various phases in the relationship
between American society and American films. But before
coming to this historical survey, let us consider the relationship as it is today--a useful contrast to what will be revealed
as being the case earlier.

I contend that increasingly of late films are telling the
truth about America, sometimes even a truth the majority
have yet to acknowledge. To select a theme to illustrate this
is tricky. As Arthur Knight has pointed out (Saturday Review,
October 2, 1971), the cinema suffers from cultural lag.

> By the time the movie medium gets around to an-
> alyzing some facet of the contemporary scene, the
> focus of concern has shifted elsewhere. When the
> movies were offering their campus rebellion cycle,

for example, that rebellion had already shifted to another phase, and the pictures themselves seemed dated, unsympathetic, and out of touch.

The same is true of films about drugs, and Knight opines that movie makers are somewhere pondering films on Women's Liberation. His explanation is that movies take at least 18 months to pass from script to screen--longer if the movie is based on a book which in its turn would have had a gestation time equally long, if not longer. We may be able to find other reasons for the lag when we come, later in this chapter, to examine Gans' account of the relation between the movie maker and his audience, an account which should help explain how things can go wrong between script and screen as well as how they can go right. I therefore pick to serve as an example not one movie, but a continuing cycle of them.

Case Study: Films about Marriage

Much of the most interesting work in the American cinema has been done within the basic genres: private eye, Westerns, gangster-spy, horror, musicals, war films, science fiction. Within each genre there are cycles. These are usually stimulated by a movie that does something new or unexpected with the genre. Other picture makers then try to follow its example, in the hope of repeating its success. One little-studied genre is the comedy of sexual manners. Hardly known before the twenties, this genre became a popular one in the hands of Cecil B. DeMille, among others, and made stars of Clara Bow and Gloria Swanson. During the thirties, a cycle of so-called "sophisticated" sexual comedies came and went. During the forties and fifties the genre comedy of sexual manners spluttered on, but in no clearly defined cycles.

In this section we shall look at another cycle that began in the mid-sixties and which rapidly became a vehicle for social commentary. This was the comedy of sexual manners crossed with the examination of married life.

My general contention about the coming and going of cycles, which this case study is intended to illustrate, is that they are replete with sociological significance. Sometimes the mores portrayed in a cycle will be in advance of the generally accepted standards of behavior in society (for example, twenties films about "fast women"). At other times,

the mores will be behind general social practice (for example,
D. W. Griffith's Victorian heroines in contemporary settings,
or the patronizing portrayal of the Negro). Still other cycles
will show mores that accord pretty well with actual practice
in the society at the time. To my mind, no simple explanation of these avant-garde, arrière-garde, or in-step relations
between what is portrayed on the screen and what is going on
in fact is likely to be found. Social changes in the nineteen-
twenties and nineteen-thirties might explain the vogue for
"daringly" advanced comedy. In times of change experiment
is easier. What will explain old-fashioned screen mores in
periods like 1910-1920 (and perhaps even the nineteen-forties)?
What will explain cycles in which the films are pretty well
geared to reality (the period 1898-1908, perhaps the nineteen-
fifties)? Explanations like, "Crazy happenings in the world
(prosperity followed by crash followed by depression) give rise
to crazy comedy," are just too glib. They give us no clue as
to how the causal connection alleged between whatever state
mores are in and the state they are portrayed as being in on
the screen is effected. An evasive answer sometimes given
is that the audience liked crazy comedy because it resonated
with the crazy state of the world (which was trying to maintain a pretense of normality). Hence the effecting of the causal connection need not be discussed. Movies are produced
in great quantities, this argument goes on, just as are pop
discs, different entrepreneurs trying anything that occurs to
them and to their hired talent. From this proffered array
the public selects what pleases it, the entrepreneurs ration-
alize their efforts, and a new cycle swings on its way.

Certainly this explanation is better than those which
suggest that movie makers foist their own predilections on a
reluctant public by persuasive advertising. But I am not fully
convinced, even though I have already said I have myself no
clear answer to offer and am not at all hopeful that one can
be found. The problem of the direction and mechanism of
causality between film and society is neglected and unsolved.
For one thing, Los Angeles has never been typical of American society, indeed California has often been thought of as
the vanguard of America. In so far as Los Angeles mores
found their way into films these would be untypical; yet most
Angelenos, and especially those in the movie community, were
recent immigrants from other parts of the Unites States: if
their mores had been fed into movies they might well have
been typical. Large-scale historical events could hardly but
influence the filmmakers, and we know that in at least one
case, World War II, direct government pressure was put on

Hollywood to "contribute to the war effort. " Political events
are muddier water. The Depression and the New Deal are
certainly alluded to in Hollywood movies: interesting would
be detailed comparison of studio output under a staunch Re-
publican executive like Louis B. Mayer at MGM, and an e-
qually staunch Democrat like Jack L. Warner of Warner Brothers. Some actors, directors and writers were liberals, others
were conservatives: these comparisons would also be useful.
That so much of American reality is critically reflected in
the films of all periods is obviously a result of the complex
interaction of audience tastes and predilections, the ideas put
up to their bosses by the creative personnel, and the guesses
about commercial potential by those bosses. There may not
have been many fast women in America when Hollywood was
making films about them. There may even have been much
disapproval of the whole idea. But there were plenty of customers curious enough to pay to see movies about them, so
they went on being made. It was this pandering (as those
who disapproved saw it) by Hollywood to the curiosity of its
public about controversial topics, and especially sex and crime,
that finally resulted in uniting the forces of moralism (notice:
I do not say "morality") behind censorship. However, they
were trying to hold back a wall of water with their hands.
Divorce and promiscuity went on in Hollywood even if they
were expunged from movies after 1934, and despite this,
they were to spread throughout the population at large.

One sacred cow in movies since the year dot has been
marriage. In the vast majority of American movies up until
recently there has been no attack on or ridiculing of marriage
in itself. Good marriages were shown as idylls. Troubled
marriages were shown righting themselves. Marriage was
portrayed as an institution within which people found emotional and sexual satisfaction. Something like this is still true
of television. But there have been changes in the movies.
A somewhat less rosy and uncritical view of marriage was
created by the cross-breeding of the irreverent and iconoclastic comedy of sexual manners with the subject of marriage.

The cycle of films about marriage I shall discuss has
been underway for some time (since the mid nineteen-sixties)
and is by no means over (during the writing of this book several films have appeared which warrant discussion). It is a
cycle of films about the condition known as married life,
once the be-all and end-all of every young American's aspirations. Its interest is that over a short period we can

see American movies changing from systematic distortion of
American society, to making serious attempts to get nearer
the truth by being more honest and critical, until they are
on the verge of going too far--in this case, despairing of all
relations between the sexes.

Put roughly, the traditional middle-American view of
marriage as we see it in movies of the nineteen-forties and
nineteen-fifties was this. Women were precious objects men
looked up to and fell in love with for life. Marriage was
conceived of as a lasting partnership between a man and a
woman truly in love, entered into for the purpose of solem-
nizing that relationship. Marriage was the central institution
of American society, the basic emotional unit, social unit,
economic unit and, when blessed with children, kinship unit.
Despite comedies of sexual manners between the unmarried,
ridicule of hen-pecked husbands, and other sidetracks, the
mainstream of movies in this period commended love and
marriage to their audience. Viewers were implicitly told
that this was how America was; or, if not that, then this
was how the best in America was; or, if not that, then this
was how America ought to be.

Curiously, in the literature of content analysis of
movies, no attention has been paid to this central theme of
marriage. While Martha Wolfenstein and Nathan Leites
(1950) have a long discussion of family life and the relations
between the sexes, they say almost nothing about marriage.
They do not discuss American men's idealization of women;
American men's misogyny and preference for the fellowship
of the locker room; or the belief that women are always trying to lure men into marriage, which men regard as a trap
until they are caught, when they realize it is what they always wanted. Marriage turns out to be a tender trap, because nothing is better than the love of a good woman. The
omission is all the more surprising since marriage connects
up with one of Wolfenstein and Leites's major themes, the
"good-bad girl." The man on the verge of being trapped into
love and marriage by a girl needs desperately to know whether
she is good or bad. A great deal of tension and interest is
generated by allowing the really good girl to come on in the
first instance as though she were bad. Ultimately the tension
is relieved by a completely innocuous explanation of all her
"dubious" actions. Adding marriage to this analysis allows
a proliferation of categories. Without pretending for a moment to match the skill or depth of Wolfenstein and Leites,
let me sketch some of this in. We could introduce categories

like the Reluctant Bachelor, the Reluctant Virgin, Chasing
the Wrong Guy, and Struggling to Get Free.

The Reluctant Bachelor is a handsome, successful
young man, who seems to have a splendid sex life without
benefit of marriage. In The Tender Trap (1955), as played
by Frank Sinatra, he handles girls easily until aspiring young
actress Debbie Reynolds sets her sights on him. Finding her
eminently resistable at first, he ultimately succumbs happily.
In Pillow Talk (1959), as played by Rock Hudson, he has a
tricked-up apartment and a wooing song he sings over the
telephone. Challenged by Doris Day's hostility (they share
a party line), he contrives to get her to fall in love with
him, and even to agree to a naughty weekend in Connecticut.
Subsequently, when they quarrel, he realizes he has fallen
for her. Other examples are Come Blow Your Horn (1963),
with Sinatra again as an aging playboy--the despair of his
Jewish Mama and Papa--who, after being clobbered by a jeal-
ous husband and out-paced by his younger brother, settles for
marriage to Barbara Rush and a stake in the family wax fruit
business, and Under the Yum Yum Tree (1964), which has
lecherous Jack Lemmon leasing his Centaur Apartments only
to nubile young females on whom, we are led to believe, he
then preys. A young couple attempting a platonic trial marriage move in and he alternates leering attempts to observe
what he imagines is going on with stabs at seduction. In
How to Murder Your Wife (1965), to which we shall return
shortly, something like the high pitch of the Reluctant Bachelor theme is reached. Not only is the bachelor life portrayed as totally fulfilling and luxurious, it is explicitly expounded
and defended during conversations Stanley Ford (Jack Lemmon)
has with his married lawyer friend Harold (Eddie Mayehoff).

The Reluctant Virgin usually goes together with the
Reluctant Bachelor. Usually the Bachelor wolf is trying to
get the Virgin into the premarital bed, but she is holding out
for marriage. Doris Day made a series of very successful
comedies in which she practically patented this role while
partnered by Rock Hudson (Pillow Talk 1959, Lover Come
Back 1961, Send Me No Flowers 1964), Cary Grant (That
Touch of Mink 1962), James Garner (The Thrill of It All
1963, Move Over Darling 1963), and Rod Taylor (Do Not
Disturb 1965, The Glass-Bottomed Boat 1966). The variations go like this. In Pillow Talk Doris shares a party line
with a wolf, and is always overhearing his conquests. Meeting her by chance, he poses as a Texan and decides to try
to conquer her. Before he does she finds out who he is, but

they get together in the end. In Lover Come Back Doris
and Rock are advertising executives. She manages to saddle
him with a name for a product but no product. Again she
falls for him under the illusion he is someone else, and a-
gain marries him. After one night she annuls, only to enjoy reconciliation nine months later. That Touch of Mink
has her fall for a tycoon, and go off with him on what used
to be called a "dirty weekend" to Bermuda. But the first
night she breaks out in spots, and the second she gets drunk.
When finally he marries her, he breaks out in spots. The
Thrill of It All is realizing that life with her gynecologist
husband is more important than her television career. Move
Over Darling reverses roles as Doris, long thought dead,
schemes to prevent the consummation of her husband's remarriage. In Send Me No Flowers she has a hypochondriac
for a husband who she suspects of having an affair, when all
he is doing is planning his own demise and trying to find her
a new man. Do Not Disturb has Doris again married, but
to a husband often away on business. She has a fling with
an Italian, but passes out drunk before anything happens.
Looking for her husband at a convention, she gets into bed
with the wrong man, and is chased half way round the hotel
before finding her husband's bed. In The Glass-Bottom Boat
she is wooed by her boss, who then suspects she is a spy.
She plays up to this, but all turns out right and as it should.

Both the Reluctant Bachelor and the Reluctant Virgin
categories endorse the same idea: premarital sex is for
men to enjoy and women to avoid; indeed, unless they avoid
it the goal of marriage will be harder to achieve. The Reluctant Bachelors, clearly, are not getting the rich sex life
they so much enjoy from the Reluctant Virgins. From which
women are they getting it, then? These women are never
the subjects of forties and fifties films, comic or otherwise.

Instead we get a group of films also in the same period
(1955-1965) we might call Chasing the Wrong Guy. In these,
the woman is predatory and sometimes offers sex to the man
she thinks she wants. A Good Guy often appears to bail her
out, even though she is No Longer Pure, or the ostensible
Bad Guy will be reformed by her love, devotion, accident,
illness or whatever. Examples are Love with the Proper
Stranger (1963), where pregnant Natalie Wood seeks out one-
night-stand Steve McQueen to help procure an abortion, and
The Apartment (1960), where elevator girl Shirley MacLaine,
seduced and then dumped by her boss Fred MacMurray, finds
happiness with Jack Lemmon.

In the fifties Hollywood treated sex fairly gingerly, and yet allowed itself to return repeatedly to the winter-spring romance.   Here it comes into the cheerless garment jungle world of Jerry Kingsley (Frederick March) in the person of his secretary Betty Preisser (Kim Novak).   Delbert Mann directed Middle of the Night from Paddy Chayevsky's screenplay for Columbia in 1959.   March was 62, Novak 26.   Similar gaps were apparent when Humphrey Bogart (55) wooed Audrey Hepburn (25) in Sabrina (1954), when Fred Astaire (56) wooed Leslie Caron (24) in Daddy Long Legs (1955), and when Gary Cooper (56) wooed Audrey Hepburn (28) in Love in the Afternoon (1957).

All of these films end in marriage, for that is still the Happy Ending, the consummation devoutly to be wished. What is marriage itself like?   Well, it is either an idyll of family and home bliss, or a real trap from which the victim Struggles to Get Free.   Illustrative of the latter are Middle of the Night (1959), with Kim Novak falling for her middle-aged employer Frederick March; and Strangers When We Meet (1960) in which Kim Novak and Kirk Douglas, both mar-

ried to others, wonder whether they should run off together.
They don't.

      I would contend that the status attributed to marriage
in movies made after 1935 coincided pretty well with the view
taken in the respectable bulk of the wider society. Popular
American movies of this period accurately represented and
endorsed the mainstream values of middle America. Movies
were not set out to shock, outrage, or thoughtfully provoke
the audience when it came to such core values of the society
as marriage (or war, or history, or politics). Indeed, why
should they be? This was not the way their role was seen.
Strong self-censorship and control was exercised by such executives as Louis B. Mayer of M. G. M. , who insisted that
"his" movies endorse mother love and apple-pie values.
Whenever movies stepped a little out of line an outcry went
up from politicians and such self-appointed censors as the
Catholic Legion of Decency and the American Legion. A
landmark case was the suppression for several years of Howard Hughes' The Outlaw (1943, finally released in 1946), a
film in which the most outstanding attraction was Jane Russell's
cleavage. That movies had a central place in society is revealed by the extent to which they were a subject of scandal
and concern for the press and for the public at large in a
way they no longer are. This central place was reinforced
by economic sanctions. [2] Mayors, local censor boards, A-
merican Legion and Catholic Legion of Decency pickets could
bring enough pressure at the box office to force managers to
withdraw films and, ultimately, producers to modify the films
themselves. This may be putting it backwards. A few actual
cases of the exertion of pressure of this kind did occur, but
for most of the sound era Hollywood successfully preempted
such trouble by means of the Breen Office, which scrutinized
scripts and finished movies before they were shown to the
public and advised on their moral acceptability. So, the
threat of economic pressure was enough to ensure prior self-
censorship. Violence, of course, got by, because there was
no Anti-Violence Legion. Travesties of history also got by,
because there was no Historical Truth Legion. Vulgar jing-
oism got by, because... Insults to minorities and foreigners
got by, because... And so on.

      Startling indeed is the contrast today. The movies
are no longer the central mass medium. They expect to appeal only to certain (self-selected) groups. The product is
tailored and differentiated (by advertising and release pattern)[3]
to suit these groups. Woe to those who mistake one product

for another, who stumble into a violent and exciting tale of
police work and corruption like Madigan (1968), expecting a
Swedish mood piece to Mozart like Elvira Madigan (1967).
One clearly defined audience is interested in shock, sensation, outrage, the limits of decency and, above and beyond
all that, being challenged by a movie. Another, less clearly
defined audience does not want any of this but rather reassurance and reinforcement. Naturally, this former audience
is the experimentally minded, principally the adolescents and
postadolescents. Among the things they are intrigued by is
this state of affairs called marriage. They have observed
it at close quarters all their lives, know it lies in wait for
most of them, and are not at all sure that it represents the
fulfillment of their aspirations.

I must confess to not knowing whether there has been
any change in outlook since the forties and fifties. While
movies were the predominant mass medium, the greater part
of their audience were married or about to be, and it may
be that attacks on that institution would not have gone down
well. Certainly, criticism of marriage as an institution is
more widespread today, when even ministers of religion have
been heard endorsing trial marriages, where premarital and
extramarital sexual experience is ever more common, and
where overt experiments in living together, group marriages,
communes, swapping, and having illegitimate children provide
well-publicized and not very strongly disapproved alternatives.

On balance, then, I am tempted to say a real shift
in attitudes has taken place, and it is certainly the case that
the audience is different in character and in what it expects
of its movies. We will come to these changes in chapters
III and V. There is moreover the seepage of taste upwards
from the younger age group to the older. More in America
than anywhere else do older people pay attention to and even
learn from--as well as learn to enjoy--what young people do.
All of this is a radically different situation from that faced
by the movie makers of the forties and fifties. This shift
could explain why the treatment of marriage in movies (not
in all movies, by any means) has changed markedly. What
is interesting is how quickly the portrayal of marriage and
its problems changed in the course of a few years. By looking at this rapid piece of "catching up" we can see movies
exemplified as a social phenomenon, getting feedback from
the society and returning it in such positive measure as to
raise the cry of having gone too far. [4]

Anyway, let me now set out the argument in some detail. Satire on married life has of course been a movie staple for as long as anyone can remember. My argument is simply that on the evidence of a recent group of films there has developed a more merciless, funny, serious, and mature approach than hitherto. This change is connected, undoubtedly, with changes going on in society. Perhaps we can pinpoint the beginnings of change in the traditional comedy around the time of Richard Quine's How to Murder Your Wife (1965). Consider George Axelrod's plot. A happy and successful bachelor cartoonist (Jack Lemmon), physically fit, member of an exclusive men's club, living in a beautiful Manhattan town house and looked after by a devoted and obsequious valet (Terry-Thomas), gets drunk, marries an Italian fireball who pops up out of a cake, and wakes up horrified at what he has done. She overfeeds him and wrecks his elegant decor, and Terry-Thomas quits. She finally gets the message when she sees that through his comic strip he is devising a plot to murder her. Whereupon--what else?--he realizes he loves her, wins her back, wins back his valet and even fixes him up with the mother-in-law. Misogyny is rampant in this film, as is the reverence for "buddy" relationships between Stanley, his butler and his men friends at the club. Marriage is a trap into which women inveigle unwary men when they are drunk or emotionally besotted. It reduces them to a flabby jelly from which clubs and jobs are their only escape.

While many of the movies I shall discuss have strong satirical elements, I am primarily concerned with bringing out their serious side: how the state of being married is viewed--its tensions, unease, and general unsatisfactoriness. Perhaps the two most jaundiced views of marriage to be found in this cycle of films are The Happy Ending (1969), to which we shall come later, and Mike Nichols' version of Edward Albee's stage play, Who's Afraid of Virginia Woolf? (1966). In this, a college professor, George (Richard Burton), and his wife, Martha (Elizabeth Taylor), invite in for drinks a younger colleague and his wife. George and Martha then proceed to expose the searing hatreds and fantasies that bind them together. Not himself married, Albee takes an almost clinical relish in exposing the newly-married young couple to the middle-aged battling pair with their temper tantrums, cruelties and hysteria. Their marriage is a pathological symbiosis between two tortured souls, complete with an imaginary child. Vicious and horrible though they are with each other, there is a mutual need for reassurance that they exist. Marriage can be based on a fusion of hatred and dependence.

While there is no direct evidence that this film influenced the subsequent ones we shall be looking at, the airing of such views in other parts of the general culture such as the theater must be allowed to have a possible spill-over effect on the movies. If this happens, then it must be effected through the writers. Much too much discussion of movies concentrates on the director and the visual action, instead of the writer and the producer. Save for a select few, writers used to be a low-status profession in Hollywood. Ever since the voracious appetite of television created such a shortage of material, this has been much less so. Good, original, popular writers are in a seller's market. More important, writers are the movie colony's bridge to the outside world. Rosten (1941) shows how they are the single professional group in Hollywood most strongly orientated to the outside world, to the wider culture beyond movies. They are more educated, they read more, they frequently have rather wide experience. If changes are taking place in the society, if dramatists or novelists are breaking new ground, it is the writers who will transmit this to the movie colony.

Following How to Murder Your Wife and Who's Afraid of Virginia Woolf? comedy and (sometimes savage) satire seem to get the upper hand for a time. Guide for the Married Man, directed by Gene Kelly, scripted by Frank Tarloff (1967), centers on a husband (Walter Matthau) who is contemplating adultery and who gets training from his friend Ed (Robert Morse) in all the ruses necessary successfully to carry it off while deceiving his wife (Inger Stevens). He has no trouble in finding a compliant woman, but he has trouble with his own guilts. At the crucial moment in the motel room he is delighted to take advantage of an excuse not to go through with things. That an itch to adultery develops in some married men is a premise of the film (cf. the earlier The Seven Year Itch, 1955, also based on a play), explained if at all by the infantile leering at wiggling behinds in which the two main characters indulge. Again, though, as in How to Murder Your Wife, the possibility that there is something wrong with the institution of marriage itself is fudged. The audience is expected to accept the reassurance that the best cure for the seven year itch is to return to the good wife. Ed, who is a real and practiced adulterer, is punished by being caught in the act. But it should be noted that while Ed gets his comeuppance, there is nowhere the suggestion that the impulse to adultery is immoral and something to feel guilt over. Matthau's guilt is comical. The film is solely concerned with "getting away with it," and merely suggests that some men,

Marital relations Southern California style are both painful and funny in Divorce American Style. Nelson Downes (Jason Robards, Jr.) tries hard to palm off his ex-wife, Nancy (Jean Simmons) on Richard Harmon (Dick Van Dyke). Bud Yorkin filmed this Norman Lear script for Columbia in 1967.

like the hero, are too guilt-ridden to indulge in it. 5

        Funnier, although also much more bitter, is Bud Yor-kin's film of Norman Lear's script, Divorce American Style (also 1967). A divorced man, Richard Harmon (Dick Van Dyke), is reduced to penury by alimony, and is maneuvred into an affair by another divorced husband, Nelson Downes (Jason Robards, Jr.), who wants to marry off his ex-wife Nancy (Jean Simmons), so he will be free of alimony and able to remarry. At the climax, Nelson's plans are thwarted when Richard's wife Barbara (Debbie Reynolds) reveals under hypnosis that she still loves him and they reconcile; so we leave Nelson trying desperately to interest a new prospect in Nancy. There is much misogyny in this film, too, as wives are portrayed as vampires out to take all they can get. More than one sequence strikes one as scarcely funny, in particular when all the fathers are shown turning up to collect the kids of their previous marriages for their obligatory visit. The sorting out of which child stems from which liaison understandably depresses the hero.

In the following year the tone, while still satirical, becomes yet more disillusioned. Written and directed by George Axelrod, The Secret Life of an American Wife (1968) concerns a suburban housewife (Anne Jackson), worried about age and loss of sex appeal, who poses as a call girl to a client of her husband's and reaps both increased self-confidence and $100. Adultery is not only not disapproved of, it is not even punished, and those who indulge in it are allowed to benefit. Only Billy Wilder (in Kiss Me, Stupid, 1964) ever dared suggest this before in the American cinema. The year 1968 also saw the filming of Neil Simon's most acerbic play The Odd Couple. Here, two divorced men share an apartment and quickly reveal the idiosyncracies that have made them impossible to stay married to in the first place, and which soon make them unable to share an apartment any more. Their life together is a wierd meld of the fellowship of the locker room with the intimacies of connubial domesticity. One must resist the temptation to read in homosexual overtones, for the odd couple do not get on at all. Their life together is an expedient.[6]

None of the films in this cycle mentioned so far is what the purist would call an important piece of pure cinema. They are directed in a workmanlike and professional way, and effortlessly performed by experienced and well-known comedy players. In the best sense they are popular American cinema, and they succeed primarily because of their scripts. The writing is sharp and often extremely witty, despite the grim thematic undercurrents I am engaged in bringing out. One needs to notice how, gradually, the themes of becoming reconciled to marriage and of rocky marriages being repaired are no longer de rigueur. The Odd Couple implies there are some people who will always choose inappropriate partners, while adultery for profit (Secret Life) is hardly in accord with orthodox bourgeois values. This already contrasts sharply with the "happy endings" of How to

Murder Your Wife, Guide for the Married Man and Divorce American Style.

By 1969 the changes going on are overt, and serious purpose is combined with excellent, one might even say scintillating, comedy in Bob and Carol and Ted and Alice. This film was a mild sensation, and was (deservedly) extremely popular. Bob (Robert Culp) and Carol (Natalie Wood) decide after an Esalen session to get into pot, adultery and possibly "swinging." Their best friends Ted (Elliott Gould) and Alice (Dyan Cannon) are a bit sceptical. Bob confesses to Carol that he has had an affair; she is pleased he has confided in her. He returns home one day to find her in bed with Horst, the country club's tennis professional and, after initial anger, lives up to his new liberal principles by offering Horst a drink. When all this is revealed to their friends, Alice is shocked and Ted intrigued. During a weekend they all spend in Las Vegas, Ted admits that he too has "stepped out of line" while away on a business trip. Alice then proposes a swapping orgy among the four of them but, after going some of the way, they all draw back when they realize this will start something they are not at all sure they know how to handle. The incidental delights of this film (both Esalan and conventional psychiatry are savagely mocked) are immense. Yet its purpose is serious. It poses well the dilemma of the intelligent, affluent Californians. They enjoy all the material advantages, but are yet vaguely bored and dissatisfied. It was directed by Paul Mazursky from a script he wrote with Larry Tucker.

Bob and Carol and Ted and Alice was an interesting case of a split developing between the more critical and highbrow film reviewers and the audience. The film undoubtedly found an audience, for it did extremely well at the box office. Many of my students had not seen it, whereas most of my

Opposite: An example of the movies' getting ahead of the powers that be, if not the public, was Billy Wilder's Kiss Me, Stupid (1964). Made for United Artists, this film dared to make light of adultery and prostitution. The original ending was changed for the United States, and the film has yet to be cleared for television. In this scene, a local waitress-hooker, Polly the Pistol (Kim Novak), shares a love seat with Orville J. Spooner (Ray Walston) and heart-throb Dino (Dean Martin). Wilder co-wrote the screenplay with his usual collaborator, I. A. L. Diamond.

The uncertainty of not knowing what the pot and sexual revolution is getting them into is reflected in the faces of Ted (Elliot Gould), Carol (Natalie Wood), Bob (Robert Culp), and Alice (Dyan Cannon). Instead of an orgy, the script Paul Mazursky and Larry Tucker wrote for Bob and Carol and Ted and Alice ended in a fantasy. Mazursky directed the hit movie for Columbia in 1969.

contemporaries (middle-class people in their thirties) had.
On a typical day the crowds lining up to see it were young,
affluent, but not teenagers. Would it be going too far to say
that many of them were not unlike Bob and Carol and Ted
and Alice? Be that as it may, they enjoyed the film hugely.
The popular press agreed. Some reviewers, however, dis-
sented. Why did the film not follow through, have an orgy?
Was the ending a moralistic sop to convention? I do not
think this is fair. Apart from the purely technical dramatic
point that stories need an ending, a rounding off of some sort,
and that an orgy would not have been one, I think there was
a general failure among highbrow writers to grasp just how
far from conventional values this film had come. Yet, all
praise to it, while its characters were foolish, we were not
asked to believe they were foolish enough to destroy themselves. The film's authors may reject conventional morality,
but they also shrink from the extremes of permissive morality
too.

Certainly another push to the disillusion with marriage
was given by Richard Brooks when his The Happy Ending was
released early in 1970. After fifteen years of marriage we
see Mary Wilson (Jean Simmons) become blowsy and disillusioned, her husband (John Forsythe), trim and prosperous.
As Time magazine (February 2, 1970) asked, what drove Mary
to be an alcoholic, pill-popping neurotic who has to fly off to
the Bahamas to calm herself, have an affair there and, finally, decide to leave her husband? The answer: "the boozy
infidelities of suburbia, the shattering of some romantic girl-
hood dreams, the parade of horror every night on the late
news. What is stressed, underscored and bludgeoned home
is the general ugliness of married life". The film was not
a comedy, and was not particularly successful. Its title was
an explicit and ironical allusion to our theme: is a wife finally deciding to leave her husband a happy ending? Is that
what marriage really is, rather than "they got married and
lived happily ever after?" (In the final scene, the husband
is trying to effect a reconciliation.)

While it was not successful, a powerful film of this
kind can influence other filmmakers, especially screen writers, to take the theme and embroider their own variations
upon it. This sort of influence, I would maintain, is one of
the principal links in the causal chain connecting movies to
society, and can clearly be seen to be going on in the films
of our case study. Sometimes the influence is mediated by
producers who get interested in filming novels or plays on

similar themes which they might otherwise have passed over.
Anyway, whatever the explanation, marriage and its travails
becomes a major theme in a flurry of films from 1970 on:
Loving, Lovers and Other Strangers, Joe, I Love My Wife,
Diary of a Mad Housewife, Move, Taking Off (1971) and Such
Good Friends (1972). My contention is that these essentially
commercial films are rich in sociological and psychological
content, serious within an often satirical framework, and
incidentally, show how much of the best current work in the
American cinema is being done by writers rather than directors. Only Loving (Irvin Kershner), Taking Off (Milos Forman) and Such Good Friends (Otto Preminger) are by directors with any claims to artistry. As a result, the films vary
in quality. Frank Perry, for example, is a heavy-handed
director: points in Diary of a Mad Housewife are thumped
rather than made. The same is true of Otto Preminger and
of his Such Good Friends. Lovers and Other Strangers ex-
udes sentimentality and cosiness, in addition to being indiffer-
ently directed. Nevertheless, when the films are lumped together as a cycle they sustain a high level, and several are
undoubtedly top flight.

Loving is possibly the least known and yet is the most
subtle, skillful and well-handled of the bunch. Its director,
Irvin Kershner, has been making off-beat and interesting
movies since his Stakeout on Dope Street of 1958. Particularly to be relished was A Fine Madness (1966), with Sean
Connery as a working-class poet, vociferous and randy, urg-
ing middle-aged ladies to "open your corsets and bloom, let
the metaphors creep above your knees." Loving is the best
film Kershner has done. The story, such as it is, is unim-
portant. George Segal plays a commercial artist, restless
about his work, his family life, his mistress. There is no
(cont. on p. 65)

Opposite, top: Problems of the middle-aged man: sexy and
destructive young women may play havoc with one's equilib-
rium. Andrea Newman's novel Three into Two Won't Go
scripted by Edna O'Brien and directed by Peter Hall for Universal in 1969. Here, the bulbous oldster (Rod Steiger) confronts the damp youngster (Judy Geeson). This film was also
too much for television, so Universal shot additional scenes
that completely altered the meaning. Bottom: Problems of
the middle-aged woman: tension, pills and alcohol. Jean
Simmons faces the lock-up after a spell with the bottle in
Richard Brooks' film of his own bitter screenplay The Happy
Ending (United Artists, 1969).

A celebration of anarchic non-conformity and sexuality was
Warner Brothers' A Fine Madness (1966). Sean Connery
plays a horny carpet cleaner (Samson Sillitoe), whose avo-
cation is to write poetry. Here Samson's wife (Joanne Woodward) tries to restrain his good spirits. Irvin Kershner directed, from Elliot Baker's screenplay.

ending. He gets a lucrative contract, but he has deeply humiliated his wife by committing adultery in full view of the guests at a party. The film is not really "about" this. It is about the texture of daily life, about trying to be creative, and trying to be successful, about fustration and routine. The scenes at breakfast where the father is like a stranger to his wife and two daughters, his impatience with a meddlesome neighbor, the visit to look over a house for sale and the depressing unhappiness apparent in the face of the aging woman who is selling it because her marriage has broken up, the routine of his visit to his mistress, all are written and directed with close attention to detail and sensitivity to nuance. But the overall tone is bleak. The house for sale is a thirty-year trap, the hero is weak, unable to choose if it hurts anyone, his impulses are self-destructive: he gets drunk at crucial moments, including the climactic party, when his love-making with a neighbor's wife is watched by the other party-goers over closed-circuit television. There is no resolution of the problems of marriage. Neither partner is going to leave the other. In the final scene they disappear into the darkness, she ineffectually flailing him with her handbag. He is surrounded by love of various kinds, yet remains curiously inward, cut off from everyone in his discontent. His life is private and interior; we never penetrate it.

Less skillful in every way, but equally uncompromising in its jaundiced view of marriage is Cy Howard's 1970 Lovers and Other Strangers, written by Renée Taylor, Joseph Bologna and David Zelig Goodman. A series of couples are presented to us, perhaps in all, and each relationship is in trouble. Susan and Mike are students living together who decide to get married, although Mike has his doubts. Mike's parents, Bea and Frank, seem happy and content on the surface, but habit has replaced love and eating has replaced sex. Bea's view is that sex is simply an unpleasant service women have to render to men when they are newly married. Mike's brother Richie is splitting up with his wife Joan. Susan's father Hal (Gig Young) is having an affair with his wife's friend Cathy (Anne Jackson), but dissembles about divorce. Susan's sister Wilma quarrels with her handsome husband Johnny because he is no longer sexually interested in her. Susan's cousin Brenda is introduced to Mike's friend Jerry. Her idea is to get a husband, his to get her into bed; she talks herself into going to bed with him at the climactic wedding party (an Italian equivalent to the Jewish wedding at the end of Goodbye, Columbus). While everyone is drawn a little closer, none of the problems is resolved. Love, it appears,

Latter day disillusion: as the Naserema enact their body
rituals. For the successful man it is hard to adjust to do-
mesticity, and his restlessness will get him into trouble.
His blameless wife will be the victim. Here George Segal
talks to Eva Marie Saint in Irvin Kershner's Loving, from a
script by Don Devlin. The Columbia release was made in
1970.

is a brief episode when one is young, it leads people to marry, after which habit and lies take over to keep the marriage
going. If the film was sharper and more pointed, it would
be a better document than it is. Nevertheless, that almost
none of the relationships portrayed in the film is really satisfactory, that none of the characters is living out his ideals,
and that this is a popular comedy, is a remarkable shift to
have taken place in the American cinema.

Sex and its dissatisfactions are at the root of the troubles of the <u>Lovers and Other Strangers</u>. But marriages also produce children, and the problems in other films center on the dissatisfactions this means. It might seem odd to include John G. Avildsen's <u>Joe</u> in a survey of recent films about marriage. Ostensibly, <u>Joe</u> is about the generation gap. But one of the gulfs between the generations is their different attitudes to marriage and indeed to the entire spectrum of sexual relations. Two married couples appear in <u>Joe</u>. Bill and Joan Compton are prosperous and upper middle class; Joe and Mary Lou Curran, working class. Both men and their women are bored into routine. When Joe comes home from work at the factory he and his wife discuss what has been happening on the soap operas, while Joe overeats. Bill and Joan exist on a fine edge of tension. Both families have "lost" their children. Joe's boys are never seen, but it is hinted that they may be motorcycle thugs, kicked out of home because, as Mary Lou says, they wouldn't stand by the door and salute when their father returned from work. The Compton's daughter, Melissa, lives in a sordid East Village apartment with a hippie drug peddler. The most exquisite nuances of class are brought out when the Comptons visit the Currans for dinner: Joan's frozen politeness and condescension, Mary Lou's cozy efforts to be friendly while serving take-out Chinese food, the inability of the women to relax despite the men's rapport (Bill has deliberately taken Joe to a bar where ad execs hang out and introduced him as the firm's new vice-president). But none of this is satire, this is life seen, as Joe puts it, as "a crock of shit." Both Joe and Bill feel the urge to hit out.

The film, written by Norman Wexler, is not really partisan to either side of the generation gap. Marriage may be pretty unsatisfactory, but what are the children replacing it with? What Joe's children are up to is not shown, never mind endorsed, while the grubby, evil life of Frank and the other drug-using kids is made very repellant indeed. Does the film hint that marriage and the privatized family life in which it is embedded create between them the sick reactions of the children? One may raise the question, but the film does not give an answer. The film does have a dramatic end that one can see coming a mile off. Robbed by hippies, Joe and Bill hunt for them, taking guns along just in case. Joe starts shooting while Bill watches and when, finally, Bill shoots, who should he gun down but his own runaway daughter Melissa? The ending is done with a freeze-frame, leaving us to ask, "What next?" Such questions, "What next?," "Is

Middle-aged lovers rendezvous in the toilet: a panorama of
married and unmarried couples were satirized in Lovers and
Other Strangers. Here Gig Young and Anne Jackson suffer
another interruption. This Cinerama release was directed
by Cy Howard from a screenplay by Renée Taylor, Joseph
Bologna and David Zelag Goodman. The message for 1970
was that most sexual relationships are unsatisfactory, so
laugh.

there no way out?," and the implication in the lack of answers that there are no answers--this now becomes the de-
pressed mood of the cycle.

I Love My Wife, directed by Mel Stuart, written by
Robert Kaufman, reverts to the issue of sex versus love,
with offspring a mere background noise. It traces the breakdown of a marriage brought about by the husband's juvenile
obsession with sex and his wife's lack of interest in it. Nar-
rated by means of home movies and flashbacks, the film tells
how Dr. Richard Burrows (Elliott Gould) develops his sexual
obsessions early, marries a pretty but ordinary girl, Jody
(Brenda Vaccaro), gets imprisoned in suburbia with kids, a

wife getting fat, dowdy, and indifferent to sex, and, finally, suffering his mother-in-law to move in. He has an affair with the wife of a patient (Angel Tomkins), but confesses to Jody about it, and she then tries to commit suicide. Richard rebels, packs off his mother-in-law, sends Jody to a reducing farm--but it all doesn't work. At the end he has moved out and pursues sexual adventure by making casual pick-ups in bars, while Jody seems to be getting along well with a mature and prosperous man whose sexual demands will clearly be less than Richard's.

It is difficult to know what this film's point of view is. For Richard, marriage and children are a frustrating (rather than a tender) trap. His need is to be promiscuous. Jody prefers food to sex, but is shocked by Richard's peccadilloes. Jody may be happier with an older and more mature man. Richard is certainly lonely and aimless as he engages in casual sexual conquests. Perhaps we are being told that the problem is his immaturity (an Elliott Gould speciality as Bob and Carol and Ted and Alice and Move testify), or the immaturity of Americans in general with regard to sex. Bob and Carol and Ted and Alice and the later Carnal Knowledge seem to push the idea that Americans are sexually confused and immature, and have only become aware of this when suddenly let loose in the jungle of freedom and experimentation. The basic confusion is of course between sex and love, leading to persistent attempts to forge a link between them (i.e., idyllic happy marriage), and the resultant disappointment and sense of entrapment when marriage turns out to be a prosaic and unsatisfactory affair.

Romantic love is an ancient enough notion, although there have always been sceptics who doubted whether it really existed. Be that as it may, romantic love was originally something quite separate from and indeed necessarily outside marriage. That was the basis of much of its attraction. It was either something unmarried girls pined away with, or else it was something that sorely tempted respectable married ladies. A marriage based on love was an unusual thing, hence Othello, hence the tragedy of Romeo and Juliet. In much of Europe, even today, marriage is viewed as a legal or financial necessity, a social obligation rather than a personal decision; whereas a married woman's taking an aptly named "lover," a man a mistress, are matters of the heart. One of the changes the philosophy of egalitarianism has brought about in Western civilization is the notion that love, and sex based on love, is the only proper basis for that most prosaic of all institutions, marriage. That love may be confused with infatuation, that love may not last a lifetime, that love itself may be an illusion--these dangerous suggestions have been ignored. Only in the present century is America having to come to terms with all this, in its popular arts as well as its intellectual understanding.

For long, America had the worst of both worlds. Puritanism discouraged extramarital love and sex while religion colluded with social obligation and sexual need to promote marriage. Instead of being the ritual endorsement of the important social institution of marriage, religion through a sense of personal duty and conscience encouraged an idealized fusion of love, sex, happiness and marriage.

It may be thought that the argument about the felt personal obligation to seek love and sex only in marriage ignores the relative ease with which divorce can be obtained in some states and the high divorce rates which indicate that people take advantage of this way out. Marriage is thus not a trap, for if it is unsatisfactory it can be dissolved. This does not at all show that Americans have separated love from marriage, however. Indeed, one might well turn the argument around. The high incidence of divorce can itself be explained by people's belief that romantic love and marriage should go together and that when they do not something is wrong with the marriage. Most divorces take place precisely because the spouses find they are no longer "in love"--if they ever were--or have fallen in love with others. After divorce their aim is usually to remarry, perhaps uttering that giveaway phrase, "this time it's the real thing."

The real what, one asks? Real love and therefore real marriage, comes the answer. It deserves to be noticed that movies peddled this message off screen as well as on. Long before divorce was as common as it is now, society continued to idolize stars who married and divorced each other frequently, each time justifying their actions, both divorce and remarriage, with reference to love, its lack, and its rediscovery. The first time a big star did this, Mary Pickford in the nineteen-twenties, the country was scandalized; but familiarity breeds acceptance.

At all events, one of the subtler things about several of the movies in this cycle is what I have called the symbiosis that develops within an ostensibly unsatisfactory marriage (Who's Afraid of Virginia Woolf?, The Odd Couple).

Hence divorce is not really available as a solution. This seems to be what is going on in Frank Perry's film (1970) of Sue Kaufman's novel, Diary of a Mad Housewife. There is some slight suggestion of sexual immaturity (Jonathan Balser's inept pleas for "a little ol' roll in de hay"), but it is only incidental. Jonathan's wife, Tina, gets pushed around by him, by their children, by life in New York, by the whole status race. Quietly going mad, she begins an affair with an attractive writer. But, though it is good sex, he turns out to be egocentric, inhuman and perhaps even perverted. Tina, it seems, is a born victim. She breaks off with him and is about to do so with Jonathan, when financial disaster strikes and Jonathan breaks down and becomes a dependent child again. She cannot resist. Her refuge is group therapy. Poor Tina! Money, children, a Phi Beta Kappa from Smith, good looks, and yet she has married a man who turns out to be a child in need of a mother, and she takes a lover who turns out to be a monster. Her children, despite Spock applied with intelligence, are insufferable prigs.

Although directed by a man, this is perhaps the first film of the cycle to look at marriage from the point of view of the woman. Also, it is the only one written by a woman. Much of the power and conviction of the film stems, as with all those discussed so far, from the performances. Richard Benjamin's childish, petulant and willful Jonathan is a masterful creation. Carrie Snodgrass's Tina makes the heart of every male in the audience ache to sweep her away from it all. Marriage is again pictured as a symbiosis between two balanced, mutually dependent yet ultimately self-destructive forces. Alternative arrangements and satisfactory resolutions do not exist. The participants must simply build new compromises, shore up tottering structures.

A brief respite from despondency is provided by Move, directed by Stuart Rosenberg, written by Joel Lieber and Stanley Hart. In Move, as in Joe, marriage is not the ostensible theme; in fact the theme may be something to do with appearance and reality--what is, and what is imagined. Move chronicles a few days in the life of a writer and his wife. Hiram Jaffe (Elliott Gould) writes pornography for a living. His wife Dolly (Paula Prentiss) is a nervous girl, wanting a child; more immediately, she wants to get their household move over with. She tries to keep calm in the face of menacing phone calls from a mysterious moving man who seems out to frighten them. Hiram's sexual fantasies interrupt the narrative. At one point he has a prolonged sexual bout with an English

girl, of whom he can find no trace when he revisits the building. The move is made, despite surrealistic upsets with wall
paint, a chase with the local unfriendly cop, and the theft of
all their furniture. At the end they play happily in the bath
of the empty apartment, like a couple of kids, with the dog
looking on. There is no ending really. Things will probably
go on much as before. Both are still young, they like each
other, he still has the yen to stray out of line, she hankers
to settle down.

     This last bunch of films appeared in 1970, which
means they were conceived and written during the years 1967-
69 at the latest, a period when America's mood was at its
darkest, political polarization and generational revolt at its
bitterest. By the following year, 1971, there are traces of
mellowing, the transformation of horror and tragedy into the
normal and commonplace. Taking Off means, of course,
running away from home. Early in 1971 Sally Field ("The
Flying Nun") starred in a poignant movie for television on
the same theme entitled Maybe I'll Come Home in the Spring.
She is young and has taken off. The story begins as she returns to her bewildered and hurt parents and envious younger
sister. The privations, deceptions, and pointlessness of her
flight recur to her in flashbacks as she readjusts to home and
tries to communicate with her sister. Her boyfriend turns up
and tries to make her choose between him and her parents.
She stays with them. She finds her parents searching for her
sister's drug cache, to protestations of innocence. When she
comes across it herself she tries to talk some sense to her
sister, only to be bitterly rebuffed as a repressive, interfer-
ing force. At the end, the younger sister is taking off.

     The norm in many of these movies, for no other rea-
son than to enable the scriptwriter to center on social psychology rather than economics or politics, is to make the
parents intelligent, socially established and comfortably off.
They are nonetheless very tense and confused about what is
happening (except when no tension is required, i.e., in a
comedy). In Taking Off even this deviation from the "norm"
is given up; the parents in the film (Buck Henry and Lynn
Carlin) are genuinely nice and well-meaning. The movie
operates with very little tension at first: a singing audition
and home life are intercut. They come together when we
learn that their daughter is out at an audition but is thought
by the parents to have "taken off." When she comes back
and a hassle develops she really does take off. Her parents
are lured off into upstate New York thinking their daughter

has been found, only to discover it is their neighbor's daughter, also a runaway, who has given the police a false name. They join the Society for the Parents of Fugitive Children, which stages elegant formal dinners with speakers, celebrates returnees like Biblical Prodigals, and even has a trial session with marijuana. This leads to a session of strip poker with another couple, which the returned daughter sees. At the end her hirsute young man is brought over for dinner to meet the parents and, though he says little, he eats heartily and confesses to a huge income as a musician. He comments how funny it is that he writes songs to protest things and most of his earnings go in taxes to finance what he is protesting against.

Such tension as there is, then, comes from the confused society in which the drama is set. Once again, the middle-aged years of marriage are seen as a routine that can ill conceal boredom and restlessness. Perhaps the restlessness rubs off on the children to the extent that they feel the need to "take off." At one point our hero identifies someone else's runaway daughter and, after a fruitless chase, almost manages to get an affair going with the mother. And through all of this he remains a harmless, decent, rather weak man. Perhaps the facts that the director, Milos Forman, was a recent refugee from Czechoslovakia, and his script was by a team, account for the off-beat structure and treatment.

Taking Off, then, joins the other films in nagging away at the lost sexual basis of marriage, the reluctant, guilty search for sexual satisfaction outside of it. Only in Bob and Carol and Ted and Alice is it allowed that sexual life in marriage can be reasonably full, and there it proves insufficient to stave off boredom and restless experiment. Love and sex having once been fused when the marriage began, the partners seem unable to unfuse them and accept the responsibilities of marriage while seeking sexual pleasure elsewhere. I take it that these films were--inarticulately, to be sure, since popular film is not a didactic medium--pointing the accusing finger at marriage itself, the ideal versus the institutional reality. People expect too much of marriage, we are being told; they use it for false purposes like possessiveness or masochism, do not mature within it, victimize their children because of it, and so on. This is not universal, of course: hints have been dropped that the false institution is flawed by a basic sexual maladjustment in both men and women (rather than that marriage causes the maladjustment).

Whether stimulated by the novel Portnoy's Complaint (1969)
or not, I do not know, but Carnal Knowledge (1971) is a bitter and disillusioned film on this theme. Its heroes are middle-aged and hence had their sexual initiation in the forties
and fifties, the heyday of the myth of love and marriage mentioned at the beginning of this chapter. It begins as two college roommates discuss their sexual dreams--and thus em-
phasizes the old ethos of marriage. We follow them as they
both have an affair with the same, seemingly innocuous girl
(bad-good rather than good-bad). One, Jonathan (Jack Nicholson), is lecherous and fickle, the other, Sandy (Arthur Garfunkel), serious and devoted. The girl, Susan (Candice Bergen), loves the lecher but can't hurt the devotee (out of weak-
ness, not kindness), so, bitterly, the lecher breaks off with
her. He later comes across his dream woman, in the person of Bobbie (Ann-Margret), perfectly built, compatible, a-
doring. While Sandy has married and had a family by Susan,
Jonathan is shacked up with Bobbie. Both arrangements go
wrong. Sandy brings his current, rather domineering mistress to Jonathan's house and a swap is proposed, but Bobbie
tries to commit suicide, while the mistress walks out in disgust. At the end Jonathan recalls his affairs, while Sandy
has blossomed into a moustachioed, be-jeaned trendy, with a
little nineteen-year-old draped around his paunch. He is still
idealistic and serious, Jonathan is still cynical. But in fact
Jonathan lives in illusion too, being able to manage sex only
if an ego-building, male-domination fantasy is repeated, word
for word, by a certain prostitute.

This film tells us that a whole generation in America
is sexually screwed up; that no matter what direction they
take in life, they are in the grip of destructive sexual fantasies that cannot be fulfilled. It is a morality play through
and through. Its didacticism makes the viewer want to challenge its makers by saying, "Well, how does your attitude to
sex differ from that of Sandy and Jonathan--where lies the
sexual satisfaction and peace you have achieved so that you
can sneer at others; how did you transcend your upbringing?"

Opposite: College disillusion: Sandy (Arthur Garfunkel) loves
Susan (Candice Bergen). She will eventually marry him, although she really loves Jonathan (Jack Nicholson). Jules Feiffer wrote a painful script of how relationships begun at college will mess up the whole of later lives. Carnal Knowledge
was directed by Mike Nichols for Avco Embassy in 1971. The
film was a breakthrough in sexual frankness and made a very
considerable amount of money.

High School disillusion: the teasing but available Jacy (Cybill
Shepherd) enjoys being the talk of the town, and will elope
with Sonny (Timothy Bottoms), only to have her parents break
it up.   When The Last Picture Show is over, so will be adolescence, school, innocence, small-town life.   Peter Bogdan-
ovich directed for Columbia in 1971, coauthoring the script
with the author of the original novel, Larry McMurtry.

Mike Nichols, the director, and Jules Feiffer, the writer,
are of the same generation as that which they portray so
scathingly.   By implication to condemn a generation so sweep-
ingly is all very well, but we are also invited to laugh, to
feel superior, to feel pity but in a superior way, as though

we know something that Sandy and Jonathan's generation did not, as though we have broken out of the traps and hang-ups they experienced. But have we? The movie invites us to indulge in the same sort of self-deception it exposes. Works of art with such a tendency are vulgar.

Later in 1971, The Marriage of a Young Stockbroker ended up by suggesting that, since being married messes up people's relationships, the only solution is to be together without marriage. Bill (Richard Benjamin) is a compulsive voyeur: bottoms, porno-movies, girls in bikinis, he loves to spy on them. Married to a beautiful girl, Lisa (Joanna Shimkus), he somehow can't bring his erotic fantasy life and her together. Sexed-up after a dirty movie, he determines to rush home and get her into bed without delay. Confronted with her laying the dinner table, he finds inane small talk coming out of his mouth. After having casual sex with a pick-up he attempts to return to the girl's apartment to arrange another meeting. When she opens the door all he can manage is a lame excuse about forgetting his wallet. His wife Lisa leaves him after catching him ogling some girls and goes to stay with her sister Nan (Elizabeth Ashley), who is fascinated by Bill's voyeurism. Lisa's deeper reason for leaving Bill is that she feels powerless married to him and his oddity and the dull domestic grind; she finds solace only in the fantasy of taking a job modeling in New York. Confronted with a female psychiatrist who seems to have cowed his brother-in-law (Adam West) and who is to treat his voyeurism, Bill rebels. Returning to Lisa with a Mexican divorce, a confession about the pick-up, and the news that he has quit his job, he carries her off again. Her sudden turnaround is not really explained except by her new freedom of choice. The "happy ending" is not up to the standards of disillusion that earlier films in the cycle have set.

The cycle gradually fades away. Otto Preminger's 1971 film Such Good Friends (written by "Esther Dale," a pseudonym for Elaine May), portrays the disillusion of a married woman who, during what turns out to be her husband's last illness, discovers just how unfaithful he has been, whereupon she decides to get her own back by herself sleeping with their "good friends." In the same year, One Is a Lonely Number, directed by Mel Stuart from a script by David Seltzer, also focusses on the woman's angle. Amy Brower (Trish Van Devere) is walked-out on by her professor husband. The rest of the film is a chronicle of her trying to get over him, striving to cease being dependent, all of this symbolized in

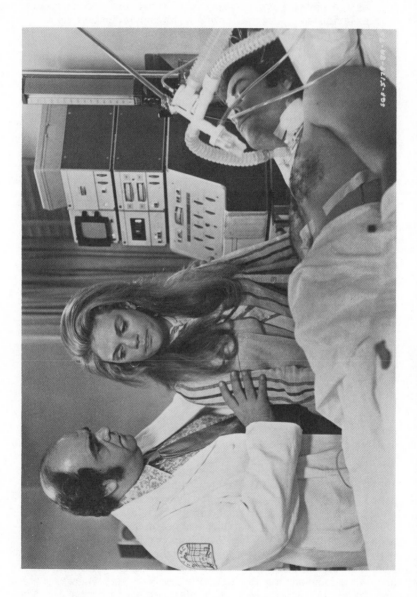

her new job as a lifeguard.   Marriage, in these last films,
is something women have to overcome.   Such a philosophy
is rather too radical and it is once again Paul Mazursky who
enters the fray to bring about a sensible compromise.

Blume in Love (1973) concentrates on the storms which
may arise in marriage, but allows them to end in reconciliation.   Stephen Blume (George Segal) is a successful lawyer
whose wife Nina (Susan Anspach) leaves him when she suspects there has been hanky panky between him and his secretary.   She moves out, takes a lover, Elmo (Kris Kristof-
fersen), and spurns Stephen's entreaties.   One night he over-
powers her and they make love.   Some time later Elmo appears at his office to say that he is moving on and Nina is
pregnant.   In Venice, where they honeymooned, there is a
reconciliation.   A baby, a felt need for stability, and a basic compatability make the relationship worthwhile: Nina's
uncertain sense of who she is and Stephen's lustful appetites
drove them apart.   As in Bob and Carol and Ted and Alice,
Mazursky injects an element of common sense.   Marriage is
a much less romantic and more practical matter now, and
writers can turn to other themes.

A rounding-off of Mazursky's efforts may be seen in
Gilbert Cates' film of Stewart Stern's script, Summer Wishes,
Winter Dreams (1973).   The film is about the menopause in
men and women.   Looked at from the analytical point of view,
it is a meditation on the middle years of marriage, on preoccupation with self and death.   As a solution it offers only
greater understanding.   Joanne Woodward plays Rita Walden,
married for twenty years to an oculist, Harry (Martin Balsam).   The routines of the middle years of life, with the
children grown up, and illness and death a nearby menace,
are making Rita distraught.   Her husband seems dull and un-
feeling.   It is only when, in a visit to a Normandy battlefield,
she realizes that he too is coping with strong emotions, that
she is able to achieve some peace and understanding.   Some
critics found the film mawkish and overwrought; perhaps the

Opposite: Latter day-disillusion: When Dyan Cannon's husband's delicate condition deteriorates, despite James Coco's
ministrations, she discovers a whole secret sexual life he
had, which everyone knew about but her. Her subsequent reactions to this revelation make up the material for Otto Preminger's Paramount picture, Such Good Friends, based on the
novel by Lois Gould, adpted by David Shaber and written by
Esther Dale (1971).

subject and the philosophy were hard to accept.

This lengthy review of a cycle of films on marriage is over; it is time now to draw the threads together and show relevance to the theme of the chapter as a whole, namely the changing relationship between films and society. We have looked at a cycle of films that have reflected, criticized, idealized, and distorted attitudes towards the institution of marriage. Attitudes toward sex and marriage were in fact changing very quickly in America during this period (1966-73), and the films reflect this, carry it along, fuel it perhaps, and also point up the rationale: what was wrong in the first place. There is no way of knowing if they cause social change. But clearly, in becoming more critical of society, they join in the critical debates going on. Such debates do result in social change so, indirectly, films may contribute to it.

Two further aspects of the question remain to be dealt with. Has film always stood in the same relationship to society? And, what mechanisms and institutions effect this connection between film and society? The second will be left till last because to an extent it explains what we shall describe in response to the first question. So let us now take in an historical survey of movies' relation to society.

Historical Shifts in the Relationship of Movies to Society

In the very beginning, in the eighteen-nineties, movies were an extremely cheap sideshow kind of entertainment. Probably only a minority of the population went to them. Certainly the press and the middle class associated them with such things as vaudeville, the circus and the penny arcade. All these were lower-class distractions, ephemeral, not to be taken seriously, not even to be noticed. The movies shown were primitive "actualities" (what we would now call newsreels), faked actualities (e.g., prizefights restaged with stand-ins), and very brief stories. One can safely say that the medium traded mainly on the novelty of the fact that pictures moved, rather than trying to do anything with this

---

Opposite: Writer-director Paul Mazursky rounds out a cycle of films about marriage with Blume in Love (1973). After adultery and analysis, Stephen Blume (George Segal, right) and his wife Nina (Susan Anspach) are reunited when her lover Elmo (Kris Kristofferson) moves on.

Problems of the middle-aged couple: self-preoccupation, hysteria, the generation gap, hypochondria, the need for love.
In Summer Wishes, Winter Dreams, problems of communication with their grownup children force Joanne Woodward
and Martin Balsam back to a renewal of their own relationship, when they face their own weaknesses. Gilbert Cates
directed for Columbia in 1973, from a slightly lugubrious
screenplay by Stewart Stern.

---

potential. By the early nineteen-hundreds the novelty was
wearing off and the story film lasting one or two reels was
emerging. Georges Méliès in France made fantasies about
trips to the moon (1902); Edwin S. Porter in America in
1903 made the first Western, The Great Train Robbery (gang
robs train and is caught with the help of the telegraph); in
1905 Cecil Hepworth in Britain made the first suspense story,
Rescued by Rover (little girl is kidnapped, dog leads father
to the rescue). In 1908 the redoubtable D. W. Griffith began

Further problems of middle and old age: widowerhood and elderly parents. In I Never Sang for My Father (Columbia 1970), Gilbert Cates coped with a film version of Robert Anderson's play. Gene Hackman struggles valiantly to communicate with his aging father (Melvyn Douglas), despite the latter's mistreatment of his sister (Estelle Parsons), his possessiveness, and his indifference to his wish to re-marry. The film ends with a complete break between father and son.

his career as a director at the Biograph Co.; Griffith was the man who was to take the cinema from the crudities of the 1907 Rescued from an Eagle's Nest (eagle seizes baby, man rescues), in which he had acted, through the 1912 two-reel Western The Massacre (Custer's last stand), to the zenith of the feature silent film, Birth of a Nation (melodrama about the Civil War and its aftermath) in 1914. Gathering momentum in the early years of the century and accelerating after 1911, the cinema was becoming the popular medium of mass entertainment by World War I--a position it was to retain until several years after World War II.

Sermons, classics, current theater hits, Shakespeare adaptations, biblical epics, slapstick comedies, and Westerns were poured out before the nineteen-twenties. Much of the approach to life and manners in these films was derived from the late Victorian theater and music hall, as Vardac (1949) documents. Most stories were very moral tales, most endings happy. In slapstick comedy, however, some very revealing glimpses of mores, manners, snobberies and oppressions are given. However crude, the comedy situations were often taken from life, making the unselfconscious social background to comedies by Arbuckle, Chaplin and Keaton deserving of close scrutiny. Arbuckle and Chaplin, in their early short films, are usually working class: they play shop assistants, waiters, factory workers, policemen, convicts, soldiers, and so on. (Keaton, by contrast, is frequently the rich idiot, or the ambitious, go-ahead technician.) In these films wealthy women will disdainfully stick their noses in the air; restaurant customers bully waiters mercilessly; even policemen are afraid to move among the criminal classes who live on Chaplin's Easy Street (a rookie cop defeats the slum bullies). These films show a society deeply divided between the working class and the middle class, with a further division between the respectable working class struggling to live by values dictated by the middle class, and the criminal or simply upstart working class which does not. There is an unselfconscious authenticity to all this background, but the tensions of it are discharged by the humor.

By the late teens and twenties the cinema was becoming "respectable." In urban centers cinemas were built to cater to the "carriage trade." How was this broadening of the class base of the cinema audience achieved; what brought the carriages to the door? Film moguls had long thought that films of Shakespeare, of famous actresses like Bernhardt and Duse would do the trick. They did not, although "reverent" biblical spectacles did. The long-term answer was discovered by Griffith, perhaps influenced by the long and spectacular Italian film imports. What was keeping away the carriage trade was the short form. Once filmmakers broke out into the so-called feature-length movies (lasting one hour or more) they made an entertainment long enough to offer some competition to the so-called legitimate theater, a form which also had possibilities of carrying serious content. Slapstick shorts and serials continued to be made, but the feature film and the double-feature bill soon became standard fare.

In the period when movies were a sideshow (up to 1905) they were very short and crude and traded largely on the novelty value of pictures that moved and not on what the moving pictures could be used to convey to their audience. They took what audience they could get and were glad of it.

In the immediately following period (1905 to 1920) movies began changing very rapidly from a crude and primitive use of the medium to quite sophisticated uses. But sophisticated more perhaps in technique than in content. The staple products were one-reel and two-reel comedies, Westerns and dramas, and the level of their story content was well suited to the young, urban, working-class audience they were intended to please. They were fast moving. A long concentration span was not required. Humor was broad rather than subtle: silent film lent itself mainly to pantomime acting. As yet, movies made few demands on their audience. To explain the subsequent change that came about we need to digress briefly on the development of the movie industry.

In the twenties, thirties and forties a rather different situation developed. After World War I, movie attendance went up to very high levels, at its peak averaging in the United States something like two or three visits a week per person. When one reflects upon how averages are constructed, one realizes that the amount of movie-going which lay behind such figures, by some persons at least, must have been very great. However reliable such figures are, what they generally indicated was incontestable: a huge demand for movies. To cope with this demand a system of many theaters, at many price levels, in different neighborhoods, and specializing in all sorts of films, was developed. The variety of outlets was bewildering: first run, second run, re-run, split week, double feature, triple feature, grind house, etc. Enough movies had to be made to fill all the program slots of all these theaters. This basically strong demand was matched by various factors encouraging monopolistic practices within the industry, making it a difficult industry to enter either as producer or importer. Vertical integration of production, distribution and exhibition left little room for the truly independent producer. Since almost all movies were successful, it was difficult to "make it" simply by offering a product which was popular. Everything was popular, so monopolists used only their own product. Then they faced two major problems: how to generate sufficient product (ideas for movies do not grow on trees); and how to finance its very expensive production.

Mercillon (1953) explains these developments as follows. Early experiences of the movie business had been of a risky, capricious and fly-by-night nature. As costs rose, those in charge were risking more and more and hence were constantly searching for a secure market base against which they could plan production and obtain finance. Production companies accomplished this partly by buying theaters (guaranteed outlets for their product) and partly by block-booking (selling movies in package deals, forcing exhibitors to take movies they weren't keen on if they wanted to show ones they were keen on), and also by amalgamations and takeovers, and the formation of cartel-like coordination mechanisms between firms. As the business grew, advance planning demanded ready cash in sums that could not be raised from current revenue and the movie companies had to go to the big New York banks. This in turn led to the same banks' having interests in several, apparently competing companies. Such control did not make them openminded to newcomers trying to enter the industry.

This digression may go some way to explain why Hollywood movies became what they were. All movie production was concentrated in one place, Los Angeles, which was not a center of traditional art and culture. Power was concentrated in a few hands. Very high technical standards were maintained. And, most important, something akin to a "Hollywood outlook" developed. Renegade, off-beat filmmakers at war with Hollywood or society either came to terms or quit. None of this is to say classical period Hollywood movies are not diverse and fascinating, for they are. It is to say that Hollywood was a finely adjusted mechanism, and it became progressively better and better tuned to its audience, and it is for that reason that we must not accept the idea that Hollywood films were always conservative or centrist in social outlook. Sometimes that was the mood, sometimes not. The main thing is, America had a strong tradition of social criticism and this made it respectable to expose, denounce, and impugn. What movies supplied were a new medium, a very elaborate series of conventions and genres, and an unparalleled discipline of form which gives film content a disturbing

force. This was the medium of Birth of a Nation, a film
which gave rise to race riots. It was elsewhere to be the
medium of Nazi propaganda.

About the only chink in the monopolistic Hollywood ar-
mor was the possibility of importing foreign films. On occasion the Hollywood monopolists tried releasing the foreign
product during the thirties and forties with poor results. This
contrasts with the situation in the silent period, when imported films were simply retitled and then shown widely; or the
period beginning with Brigitte Bardot in And God Created Woman (sexy slut wreaks havoc) (1956) and with La Dolce vita
(bored reporter pads wearily in the wake of the jet set)
(1959), since which foreign films have gone down very well.
(Indeed, American International Pictures, one of the most
prolific and profitable companies of the late sixties, began
as an importer of Italian spectaculars.) The parochialism
of American audiences seems to have been confined to the
thirties, forties and fifties. In the late forties, when the
British company J. Arthur Rank was trying to crash the A-
merican market with Technicolored spectacles, there was
talk of having to dub the films into "American" for the Midwest. Part of this resistance must also have stemmed from
the lack of known stars in foreign movies; the American audience was oriented towards stars. Stars were of course under contract to producers, and the producers virtually constituted a cartel and were not about to loan out their star prop-
erties to foreigners or newcomers trying to break into the
industry. (Some stars were of course of foreign origin, but
while talent scouts may have seen their early films, American audiences had not. Result: they had to be built-up a-
gain from scratch upon arrival in Hollywood.) Bardot was
one of the first foreign stars to arouse intense domestic interest, and to have her original French films shown in America. The fact that she spurned efforts to transplant her to
Hollywood also strengthened the trend towards importing her
films. To remind the reader: other accepted foreign stars
include Rossano Brazzi, Marcello Mastroianni, Gina Lollo-
brigida, Sophia Loren, Claudia Cardinale, Catherine Deneuve,
Jean-Paul Belmondo, Jeanne Moreau, and Sean Connery among
many. Many of their foreign-made movies were in the sixties
backed by American capital. (In chapter III we return to the
end of American parochialism and discuss it in more detail.)

A crucial time in the history of the changing relationship of movies to society was the period from 1915 to 1934.
The earlier year was the date of the important Supreme Court

decision which refused to classify movies as "speech" and hence as protected from censorship or "prior restraint" by the Constitution. And 1934 was the date when the draconian and ludicrous "production code" was finally stringently imposed on the industry by itself, allegedly in order to preempt federally organized censorship. There are many studies of all this purely from the point of view of censorship (e.g., Randall 1968). The as yet most comprehensive look at all forms of pressure and control is Jowett (1976). As has been indicated earlier in this book, the period was one of intense debate as to what was the actual relationship of movies to society from the point of view of social psychology, and what was the proper relationship from the point of view of moral influence and the like, and what should be the proper legal and business relationship: in other words, the extent to which federal, state and local lawmakers should control movies.

Lewis Jacobs (1939) has described how, after about 1908, American movies, while still dominated in some ways by late nineteenth-century values and outlook, began to show social problems and especially the situation of the working class. Around 1915 the trend to respectability also had the effect of turning stories more and more towards middle-class topics. So, any thought that movies were out of step with society was quickly to pass--the middle class always, of course, identify the values of the society with their values. With two topics the matter becomes interesting: the portrayal of women and the portrayal of crime. The working class has long been interested in crime, and this taste has been catered to by eighteenth-century broadsheets and their successors. Perhaps people whose lives are hard and who are thus tempted by crime, but whose values are against it, enjoy the vicarious acting out of crime and are comforted by its subsequent punishment. Who knows? Working-class women have always been somewhat different from the middle-class ideal. Working-class women in 1910 frequently worked both before and after marriage, coped with large families and much hardship, and were by no means totally dominated by, subordinated to, or idolized by--never mind idealized by--men. To the respectable middle class, crime was anathema, and anyway was thought to be the province of the "criminal classes." Women were the gentle sex, pale and overdressed flowers, blushing at a kiss, delicately prone to illness, and, as Somerset Maugham put it, having no organs to excrete refuse.

Now the paragraph above really describes stereotypes rather than realities. But stereotypes are what popular art deals in, and popular stereotypes can realize themselves in reality (see the discussion of stereotyping in Chapter V). However that may be, up until World War I the movies displayed great interest in crime, and they portrayed women either as Victorian wallflowers or as vigorous working-class types. However, they were also preoccupied with a combination of the two themes: the seduction of innocent young girls into what was euphemistically known as white slavery. Traffic in Souls of 1913 initiated a whole cycle of films dwelling on this theme. One wonders whether it was all that common an occurrence, or whether many films were made simply because it was a sensational topic. Certainly the stress on crime and white slavery in films was an important factor in provoking the campaigns for censorship. Ellis P. Oberholtzer, the Pennsylvania censor, documents (1922) many of these films. The stress on sex repels him, the showing of crime in detail he fears will teach aspiring criminals their trade.

Still, the morality and outlook of these films did in the end endorse the values which middle America endorsed. It was after the war that things changed.

Crime films flourished in the twenties, but they were to be revitalized and become a much greater subject of scandal and concern after the introduction of sound, not so much because they didn't preach the right things, but because alongside their official message of disapproval there was a hidden or latent message of glamor: the criminal is a free spirit, vicious perhaps, doomed certainly, but nevertheless a glamorous embodiment of American frontier individualism and the rags-to-riches story. Bergman (1971) is even able to draw an extended parallel between the career of Little Caesar (as played in the film of that title by Edward G. Robinson) and Dale Carnegie's recipe for success. [7] Movies were here reflecting the absurd circumstance that Al Capone and other gangsters had practically become folk heroes in their own lifetimes, rather in the manner of such psychopathic outlaws as Billy the Kid in an earlier era. So, while it did not outrage everyone to glamorize gangsters, there were nevertheless many respectable people who pursed their lips at the idea of gangsters, and who were shocked by their being glamorized or portrayed sympathetically by popular stars. Much the same people were fighting a rearguard action to retain Prohibition. [8] Movies were ahead of the social thinking of the "drys" too. Drinking was shown approvingly in movies for years before national Prohibition was repealed.

The changes in the portrayal of women are just as revealing. The covered-up virginal innocents lasted a long time. But in films of the twenties we begin to see the "new woman." This might be dated from the predatory vampire type, who openly "vamps" (makes seductive advances to) men. It was much more striking in Clara Bow, the "It" girl, who was short-skirted, frisky, openly provocative and independently minded. She may have been interested in men, but was unwilling to be trapped by them. Once again, the type was rooted in reality. Women's rights were gaining ground after the war: suffrage, increased employment as career women, education, drinking and smoking, all were more common. Also there was the shift in their sexual outlook. The twenties was the period when women began to escape from the old Victorian myths about sex: that sex was for men to initiate and for men to enjoy, while women had to suffer it as their marital duty. Freud, Havelock Ellis and the birth control campaign of Marie Stopes aimed to free women from these myths, to encourage them to enjoy sex and to escape the enslavement to children which was for so long a consequence of a vigorous sex life. A lot of this came to permeate the films of Clara Bow and Gloria Swanson and the sexual comedies of Cecil B. DeMille. But there was a lot of resistance to these new trends, and films were to become a focus for it.

Somehow, in the popular mind, these changes, the new clothes, flappers, jazz, drinking and "having a good time," were all wrapped up in a package. One way those against it all resisted was through Prohibition; another way was through attacks on the movies, which were seen as a force encouraging, even justifying this package of unwelcome changes. Other ways lay in adherence to old-time revivalist religion, Sunday observance laws, and other moralist behavior. Of course, we must not forget that the way movies function in relation to society was abetted not just by the content of the movie stories themselves, but also by what Hollywood came to stand for in the popular consciousness. By the twenties all major film making was on the West Coast, where mixed together were self made, enormously rich and powerful businessmen; people with little education, culture, or talent, who commanded enormous sums because they were good looking; artists and intellectuals of the highest calibre who had been lured there either by idealism about the possibilities of the new medium, or by the promise of easy money, or both; and a host of ordinary Americans. They constituted a prosperous but closed community without traditions to draw on or long-established professional ideals to look up to. Hence it came in some ways to symbolize the best and the worst in America. The crassness, vulgarity and hedonism of the nouveau-riche way of life was especially visible because it was all concentrated in one Los Angeles suburb, and because this community was itself the center of much public interest and hence press coverage (or vice versa). In particular, male and female stars conducted public romances with each other with amazing frequency, and made use of the new liberal divorce laws of the West as well. Thus Hollywood symbolized the best: the American ideal of creating a new society out of nothing and being very successful at it. But Hollywood also symbolized the worst; it magnified the danger of overthrowing traditional values and morals--what replaced them was greed, hedonism, sin and cynicism. It was the former which attracted so many migrants to the West, although the forbidden attractions of the latter may have played a part; it was the latter which gained the publicity and which perhaps fuelled up those determined that some sort of check be placed on the movies and what was thought to be their pervasive and on the whole deleterious influence.

My contention would be that the Hollywood tendency to reflect the mores of a part of society which is in advance of or deviates significantly from the rest was vigorously suppressed by the strict enforcement of the production code from 1934 onwards. There is no doubt that some films got through the net, and attempts to clean up the image of Hollywood itself did not altogether succeed, but no mesh can ever be small enough to filter out everything. Certainly the degree of public and press outcry and the number of academic and legislative investigations decreased through the thirties and forties.

Movies in these decades were a pretty lucrative business, yet they were thought by some not to be bold and venturesome. The movies were said not to be very diverse. By and large it was said they aimed at a very low common denominator in the audience, and endorsed the most simplistic kind of values and attitudes (goodness and virtue rewarded, villainy punished, and sexual puritanism, unthinking patriotism and acceptance of the status quo promoted). There was said to be a homogeneity of outlook in the films which could never have been thought to be common to their audiences. America is a vast and diverse nation, embracing great differences of custom, tradition, outlook and politics. These were said hardly to be reflected in films of the thirties, forties and fifties at all. Westerns, musicals, sophisticated comedy, horror, gangster--all the great genres seemed universalized rather than particularized. Class, religion, race, education, region, sex--all the great dividers of mankind, including Homo americanus, are barely touched on (see Elkin 1949, 1954, 1955).

At first I was myself convinced by these generalizations. Since then, I have come to write an entire book such as this to rebut them. Not film by film, of course, since this is not a film history. But by suggesting the contrary and showing how it could be explained, and by a case study on films about marriage, and a later discussion on films about blacks (Chapter V), I hope to undermine the standard view. Ultimately, however, one must rely on the films. It has to be insisted upon that the following themes can be found constantly under examination in the American cinema, and not only in the work of Great Directors: social class, social mobility, snobbery, discrimination, injustice (vigilantism, lynching), power, corruption, man versus environment, success, urban life, work, moral choice, personal responsibility, trust, sacrifice, social pressures, self-deception, the life-cycle, illness, death, psychological disorder, delinquency, cowardice, heroism, authority, egalitarianism, individualism, community, democracy, violence, sex, and love.

The United States, a new nation, is always in a process of discussing itself and what it should be. Within America this is most pronounced, the options are most open, in California--or is it that the California ethos has rubbed off on the movies? When Joan Crawford claws her way from waitress to socialite in Mildred Pierce (1945), it takes place in California. In this film--often dismissed as women's magazine stuff--"false" values are attacked when her privately educated daughter turns snobbishly against her. Having herself had a hard life, Joan spoils her daughter. The depth of the daughter's corruption is only gradually revealed, as is the depth of Joan's self-sacrifice. The film opens on a murder--of Joan's ne'er-do-well husband. At the end we know her daughter did it when she realized the husband genuinely preferred Joan to herself. Joan, however, protects the daughter and tries to "take the rap" because she feels responsible: she spoiled and hence corrupted the child in the first place. Women's magazine stories make exciting and provocative films.

However all that may be, there were also economic factors at work. While the American movie industry was profitable, it continued to be insecure despite monopolistic tendencies. Run for the most part by men from the bottom of the social scale, lucky enough to be in command of the major medium of entertainment, forged in a school of hard knocks where prosperity had often disappeared overnight, the moviemoguls felt the need to please everybody. Hence they made themselves vulnerable to censorship, boycott and trade restrictions (such as the refusal of advertisers to advertise in cinemas). Pressure even came from the State Department to be careful in the depiction of foreign lands and characters in order not to give offence to audiences abroad. As a result the movies were often given a gloss of timid acquiescence towards society and its problems. Underneath the gloss American movies of these three decades were as thematically rich as the world has ever seen (Higham and Greenberg 1968). Addicts of forties movies like myself have to remember not to recommend the situation of the movie maker as it was in that period on the basis of results. Loud were the complaints about the dilution or stultification of creativity. Perhaps the discipline of regular work, the freedom of easy profitability, combined with the incredible concentration of talent, is explanation enough of the richness. 9

To a certain extent the division of movies by decades is arbitrary: 1908 (first monopoly) is significant, 1918 (Armistice), and, of course, 1926 (sound). It so happens that the thirties are marked off from the forties by several swerves in the course of events, mostly to do with war. Decisive changes occurred in American society. The war effort (1942 on) finally ended the Depression, America became an urban not a rural society, and suburbs were invented. War hit the home front more than ever before, with universal conscription, government direction of industry, rationing. Then there were the horrors of war: the suicidally tough resistance of the Japanese, revelations of cruelty and torture of prisoners of war, the news of Nazis slaughtering Jews and Slavs, and, to cap it all, the holocaust itself, the atomic bomb.

Where thirties movies were cheery and optimistic, the forties is dominated by "black" films--the mood, the characters, the wet night streets, the motivation, is all gloomy and despairing. Tough cynics like Bogart and Ladd reach their peak in these films, as do femmes fatales like Joan Crawford, Veronica Lake, Lana Turner, Lizbeth Scott.

At the end of the forties a new factor appears further to disturb the relation between movies and society. Tele-

vision. During the fifties it comes gradually to replace movies as the principal family entertainment medium. Substantial changes are made in movie technique and in the movie
industry because of it. At one point only sale to television
of their huge libraries of old films staved off bankruptcy for
some of the movie companies. Television enters the home,
hence it is convenient. It is on for long hours. After the
modest initial investment, it is free. But more important
than all this is the way it relates to its audience; a quite different way from movies. Always there, television is a comfortable routine rather than a special occasion. As a result,
its shows and stars are quite different. The serial and the
series come into their own again in a way not seen since silent films. Actors become famous not because of their glamor or their private lives, but because of their familiarity
and amiability in a situation series week after week. Whether
the setting is a family, a hospital, a police station, or a television news room, the feeling is as though a new neighbor had
appeared in the street. Not surprisingly, very few movie
stars find their way successfully into television. Not surprisingly, very few television stars successfully accomplish the
move into movies.

The epitome of the special way television relates to
its audience is the proliferation of the popular "talk shows."
These are in effect interview programs with various "interesting" people, whether in show business or politics or what not,
or who are in the news for some other reason. But the key
to the success of these shows has little to do with their "guest
list." The key is the host. Almost always male, invariably
an experienced hand at radio or some other form of show business, his role is that of the interested, detached, amused cat-
alyst. He questions, gently. He is a smooth, regular, re-
laxing guy, the sort it would be nice to spend an evening with.
We are misled into thinking it is genuinely informal and relaxed. But the shows are masterpieces of calculation and
cunning. The host is always more prominent than the guest.
The host talks at the camera as much as at the guest. The
host treats the home audience in a familiar, easy-going, in-
cluded-in sort of way. This manner has been labelled by
Horton and Wohl (1956), "para-social interaction." The audience has the comfortable illusion of being included in a human relationship--illusion because mutual interaction doesn't
exist, it is only one-way. The host is including us in an
imaginary audience, to which he is having an imaginary relationship. Milton Berle, Jack Paar, Arthur Godfrey (especially sincere and folksy), Johnny Carson, Dick Cavett,

Merv Griffin, Mike Douglas, and Dinah Shore are all masters of this approach.

This para-social relationship did not exist between the traditional movie star and his or her audience. Hollywood stars were gods and goddesses. Larger-than-life creatures of the silver screen, whose marriages and affairs, whose lives beside their swimming-pool palaces and in night-club banqueting halls, were glamorous and magical. More directly, the players in movies played parts, not themselves. In most films the star does not look at the camera, still less glance at it fondly and send wisecracks towards it. The viewpoint of the spectator, not the member of the family circle, is what characterized film-going. As experiences, then, movies and television were not substitutes for each other.

Despite this, or perhaps because of this novelty, television was a new and exciting social phenomenon, which appeared for a while to be sweeping all before it. As the coast-to-coast network system was completed, television set ownership figures grew rapidly. Before very long, the habit of staying home of an evening to view began to eat into the movie habit of attendance two or three times a week. The first audience to be captured was that of children. Early morning shows, and weekend mornings were filled with children's material, much of it cartoons and serials. This was free, shown conveniently at home where parents could keep an eye on their children, and they could play, do other things, eat and fight without interference from ushers or harassment from bullies. About the same time the family audience--those old or tied to the home with children--similarly found it convenient to get the television habit and drop the movie habit.

Complicating the situation was the final settlement of the antitrust action brought by the federal government against the major companies. Reluctantly, each of them entered into "consent" decrees, whereby they agreed to "divorce" themselves from their chains of theaters. They remained producers (manufacturers) and distributors (wholesalers). But the key to economic security is the regular flow of cash through the box office, and that was lost. Just before this blow, Hollywood was twice "investigated"--in 1947 and 1951--by the House Un-American Activities Committee. For all of this to be compounded by the growth of serious new competition was enough to put the wind up anyone.

Hollywood, naturally, was frantic. They had little

financial interest in the broadcasting networks and so stood
to gain very little from the success of television. Somehow,
the audience had to be lured back from television. One could
say that the series of gimmicks launched in the early fifties--
three-dimensions, Cinerama, stereoscopic sound, Cinema-
Scope, VistaVision, Todd-A. O. , SuperPanavision, etc. --were
a flop, that the decline in audiences and the theater closings
continued inexorably. But it wouldn't be implausible to argue that had it not been for the gimmicks, the decline would
have been faster and Hollywood would have had no time to adjust itself to the change. Economic crisis has been endemic
in movies ever since television appeared, but was serious a-
gain in the early sixties, and acute in the early seventies.
While the long-term crisis may be attributed to television,
the most recent one must be laid to imprudent investment in
poor product: colossal and repeated commercial misjudgment
by Fox, MGM, Paramount, and other studios.

Whatever the gimmicks did, however, they did not restore the habit, they did not restore the conditions that had
allowed Hollywood to aim at the lowest common denominator.
The other strategy adopted by Hollywood was more pertinent
to its problems. It set out to do in movies what television
could not do. There were financial limits to television; physical limits to the size and hence power of its screen and loud-
speaker; and subtle social limits turning on the fact that it was
not an occasion.

What Hollywood had to do was capitalize on the fact
that movies were an occasion, and to try to suit the movie
to the particular occasions and particular subcultures. At
first the subcultures were ignored and making movies even
more of an occasion was stressed. The spectacle movie became fashionable. Veterans like Cecil B. DeMille made The
Greatest Show on Earth (life and love behind the scenes at a
circus), Samson and Delilah (the strongman's revenge), Ten
Commandments (Moses leads the Jews), on huge budgets, and
with considerable success. Others copied. This sort of lavish picture, replete with stars and spectacle, hammily mixing
religion and sex, or circus thrills and sex, was beyond the
grasp of television. These spectaculars were family audience
pictures, still made for the broadest spectrum of opinion (religious spectacles had after all to be acceptable to Protestant,
Catholic and Jewish audiences). The climax of this madness
was reached in 1963 when approximately $40 million was
spent on Cleopatra (femme fatale loves and destroys leaders
of ancient Rome), an investment that is unlikely ever to be

recouped.   By way of illustrating dramatically the problems
the whole industry was in, the same company, 20th Century-
Fox, which might have been expected to have learned its lesson, also made The Longest Day (1962) (the invasion of Normandy) and The Sound of Music (the saga of the Trapp family
singers), which were smash hits.   Intoxicated by this, they
then rushed into Dr. Dolittle (1967) and Star (1968).   Dr.
Dolittle was an original musical, starring Rex Harrison, based on the Hugh Lofting tales about a man who can talk to animals.   Ever since his stage and screen success in My Fair
Lady (1964) Harrison has been expected to work miracles at
the box office.   Star was the story of the life and loves of
British musical comedy actress Gertrude Lawrence.   She was
played by Julie Andrews who, after Mary Poppins and The
Sound of Music, was also thought able to do no wrong at the
box office.   Star was even directed by Robert Wise, who had
done The Sound of Music.   Alas!   Both films were financial
disasters.   Practically every cent the studio could borrow
was poured into Hello Dolly (1969), after Barbra Streisand
was a hit in Funny Girl (1968), only to have copyright difficulties about releasing it since the original Broadway show
was still running.   Final returns were reassuring, but during
the wait M. A. S. H. (war and comedy) and Patton (war and madness) were shoring up the company.   Greater caution was apparent during 1974 when, in an unprecedented move, Fox went
into partnership with Warner Brothers to make The Towering
Inferno (how to rescue people trapped above a fire in a high-
rise).

     What Hollywood companies like Fox were desperately
trying to cope with was the fact that the long-established
"movie habit" had been eroded, and the previously docile,
if never homogeneous, audience could now be seen as divided
into quite distinct taste subcultures.   There was still a family audience, which Disney had wrapped up.   There was a
new, youth audience, of those in their late teens and twenties
to whom movie-going was an occasion, away from home and
school.   There were also distinct subcultures of middle-aged
and older people, but these were much smaller than before.
The lost audience was really lost.   The new audience was
mysterious and capricious.   In the face of this, multi-million
dollar movies made no sense: to recoup, the huge general
audience would have to be resurrected, and that was impossible.   Hence budgets had to shrink, the targets aimed at by
the movie makers had to be a little more modest.   Slowness
to catch on to this seemed to ruin most of the old Hollywood
companies in 1970 and 1971.

The movie industry took a long time to grasp that it could no longer survive by making vehicles for the values and aspirations of an imagined middle America. Television had usurped that role. To succeed now they needed once again to embody the values and outlook of advanced or deviant segments of the society and seek diverse audiences in those segments. The biggest single segment is youth. Then children. Then young marrieds. Then blacks. Then Italians, Jews, and so on. It is still possible for Airport or The Godfather or Fiddler on the Roof or The Sting or The Exorcist or Jaws or King Kong to tap a huge amalgam of these subcultures. Airport concentrates into one evening almost everything dramatic that can happen at an airport. Romance, infidelity, crime, a snowstorm, a mad bomber, a crippled plane, a hazardous landing, and so on. Several stars play what amount to cameo parts. The origin of the film is a best-selling novel. The Godfather is about the Mafia in America, and especially the disputes within the Mafia between "families." In the course of the film, "godfather" Marlon Brando dispenses patronage and tries to keep peace. His three sons are involved some more, some less. When a feud breaks out over whether the Mafia should take on the drug trade, his designated successor is shot in a moment of vulnerability. The quiet, respectable, college-educated son reveals a hidden soul of iron and settles all the/blood debts. This film also came from a best-selling novel. So successful was it that a sequel, Godfather II, was also extracted from the novel. Fiddler on the Roof is a kaleidoscope of life among Russian peasant Jews on the shtetl. It concentrates on Tevye and his family. Life, love, death and marriage are all there. The film was taken from a very successful stage musical.

The Sting (1973) was a glamorized portrait of confidence tricksters in the twenties, its appeal was the knowing complicity of the Paul Newman-Robert Redford duo. The Exorcist (1973), also from a best-selling novel, was a new twist on the horror film in that violence, gore and sex were added to religious mumbo-jumbo and things that go bump in the night. That an innocent fourteen-year old girl was the protagonist added an element of titillation. Jaws (1975) was a very traditional shocker/disaster/monster movie, gorily explicit in the modern manner, with the usual overtones about unleasing dangerous natural forces; it was brilliantly edited. King Kong (1976) was a sophisticated, heavily sold remake of a classic monster movie--fun for the whole family.

These films were huge successes, but the risks of making them (because of the initial investment) were very great. Whereas a <u>Bonnie and Clyde</u> (youth), a <u>Love Bug</u> (children), a <u>Bob and Carol and Ted and Alice</u> (young marrieds), a <u>Sweet Sweetback's Baaadass Song</u> (blacks), a <u>Lovers and Other Strangers</u> (Italians), a <u>Goodbye, Columbus</u> (Jews), a <u>Harry and Tonto</u> (old people) were relatively inexpensive.

The movies that have been successful are the movies which caught a certain audience or a certain mood and whose success bore very little relation to the amount of money spent on them. <u>The Sound of Music</u> was moderately expensive. <u>Easy Rider</u>, which made a huge amount of money, was very cheap, about $600,000. <u>Love Story</u> and <u>The Graduate</u>, separated by about three years, both of which were enormously successful, were not even that expensive. <u>M. A. S. H.</u> was also not expensive although very successful. In between was a spectacular and violent western <u>The Wild Bunch</u> which was quite expensive but quite successful. The "Billy Jack" films (<u>Born Losers</u>, <u>Billy Jack</u>, <u>The Trial of Billy Jack</u>), <u>Walking Tall</u>, and <u>Death Wish</u> far out-grossed their costs.

Above, I emphasized that today as far as the movies are concerned the primary force creating audience subcultures is age. There has of course always been age-group differentiation in American society. It has long been a source of wonder and concern to Europeans that adolescents are such a definitive and vociferous part of American culture, also an economically powerful one, with their considerable spending power. What has happened is that this teenage culture or subculture has practically taken over the movies as its favorite medium, along with rock music. Of all the subculture markets, youth is the biggest. This has finally been realized by the American movie industry and it seeks desperately to placate that market. But there has been a lack of understanding of the adolescent market and even a contempt for it in Hollywood, and this and its disastrous consequences is probably what caused the fall of the old-line studio regimes and the old guard in Hollywood during the sixties (Higham 1972).

The resort to technical gimmicks, to publicity campaigns about how "movies are better than ever" (Dowdy 1973), refusal to cooperate with television, the later resort to big-budget spectacle all reveal the pattern of an industry searching for a formula to restore lost success. The audience was thought of as a lock to which one only had to find the key in

order to turn it and have the money pour back in. For a-
while in the sixties almost anyone young or trendy, anyone
who had made a movie which could have been a smash hit
with youth, could get financing in Hollywood. Large numbers
of films like this were made in Britain by young filmmakers
with American money in the hopes that they could do what the
inexpensive Beatles films had done (Dunne 1969). All this was
a form of guessing at what the audience wants. One of the
biggest and most catastrophic guesses was the idea that young
people wanted to see movies about student revolution. A
whole cycle of these movies was made (Getting Straight, Zabriskie Point, The Strawberry Statement, R. P. M.) and they
were all unrelieved flops.

If we apply intelligence, however, certain patterns do
emerge in young audience tastes which do not lead to a formula but which help us to understand what is going on. A lot
of the most successful commercial movies of the late sixties
and early seventies in America can be divided into four main
kinds (although residue, like exploitation movies, o r The
Poseidon Adventure, Airport 75, The Sting, etc. , remain):
movies which are iconoclastic; ethnic movies; movies about
growing up, adolescence or family life; and movies and especially satires about married life. See Table 2.

Such a table makes everything look a little too neat
and tidy. What of Midnight Cowboy, Alice's Restaurant,
McCabe and Mrs. Miller, Alice Doesn't Live Here Anymore,
Nashville, Shampoo: where shall we list these? Midnight
Cowboy is about buddy-love between a cripple and a stud--
both alone in the big city. Alice's Restaurant is a gentle
film version of an Arlo Guthrie song. McCabe and Mrs.
Miller is an intense, realistic Western about the relation-
ship between a tinhorn and a whore. Alice Doesn't Live
Here Anymore is the picaresque adventures of a young widow
searching for a new life. Nashville, a political parable:
"you may say that I ain't free, but it don't worry me. "
Shampoo is a saga of the sexual stud who can't settle down.
This leaves untouched the problem of classifying Love Story,
Airport, Earthquake, etc.

Besides being commercially successful, practically
all the movies listed in the table were successful, period.
Some, but not all, are great art; all are extremely good
popular entertainment. Perhaps more significant is the fact
that they are by no means monotonously about young people.
At least not about adolescents. Only Last Summer (on the

Table 2

(Parentheses Indicate Modest
Success Rather Than a Hit)

ICONOCLASM	GROWING UP AND FAMILY LIFE
Bonnie and Clyde	Last Summer
M. A. S. H.	The Graduate
Patton	(I Never Sang for My Father)
Joe	Summer of '42
Little Big Man	(Where's Poppa)
Easy Rider	Five Easy Pieces
(Soldier Blue)	The Last Picture Show
(Drive He Said)	(The Heartbreak Kid)
Dirty Harry	American Graffiti
Serpico	Carrie
The French Connection	
The Last Detail	MARRIED LIFE
Dog Day Afternoon	
Network	Bob and Carol and Ted and Alice
	(Loving)
ETHNIC	(I Love My Wife)
	(Move)
Lovers and Other Strangers	Lovers and Other Strangers
Goodbye, Columbus	(The Happy Ending)
(Where's Poppa?)	Joe
The Owl and the Pussycat	Diary of a Mad Housewife
Cotton Comes to Harlem	Carnal Knowledge
Sweet Sweetback's Baaadass Song	(Marriage of a Young Stockbroker)
Shaft	(Such Good Friends)
(Made For Each Other)	(Blume in Love)
The Godfather	
Hester Street	

beach a girl gets raped), Summer of 42 (in a beach community boys get their sexual initiation), The Last Picture Show (adolescence ends in a small Texas town), American Graffiti (adolescence ends in a small California town), and Carrie (adolescent cruelty and revenge), are really about adolescents. The Graduate has already graduated, Goodbye, Columbus's hero already has a job. Interestingly enough, the movies, although they can be grouped together, are highly diverse. Practically all of them contain a great deal of comedy, in fact that is their predominant tone. They tend to be about people who are just a little older than the audience that will

be seeing them. (This has led to some doubling-up of the
audience because certainly many slightly older people, newly
married and still in their thirties make up the audience for
many of these films). Adolescence, as we all have found,
is a time of experiment and trying out. We perhaps see this
situation reflected in the choice of movies. Fashionable things
that are tried out these days are iconoclasm, an open and ac-
knowledging attitude towards ethnic differences combined with
an egalitarian attitude, and a tremendous interest in the nature of marriage and growing up and the emotional relations
within the family. The problem of coming to terms with parents not so much in adolescence but at a later stage, the
problems of living together in marriage, seem to fascinate
the audience for a while.

It deserves to be said that this list looks very different from a similar list that can be drawn up for the main
themes of the popular movies of the thirties; the favorites
of those days, like musicals, gangster movies, brittle artificial comedies, and Westerns, do not feature in our list.
Serious patriotic films or films which turn on whether Doris
Day will or will not lose her virginity--all these would be
ridiculous now.

Westerns, patriotic war movies, Doris Day comedies,
these belong to a time when the movies were stifled. Westerns are still made, but they are filled with a curious nostalgia and loathing (for a false past?): The Wild Bunch, Little Big Man, McCabe and Mrs. Miller, The Cowboys, Soldier
Blue, The Culpepper Cattle Co., The Shootist, Buffalo Bill
and The Indians or Sitting Bull's History Lesson reflect some
of the things presently being thought, some of the critical
self-awareness America is developing and a nostalgia for what
were once thought to be simpler times. Critically examined,
these times are shown up as brutal and degrading, not just
simple. The Wild Bunch (1969) invest enormous violence for
little reward, are hunted by equally merciless psychopaths,
and meet their apotheosis in taking on a Mexican war lord
and his entire army. Little Big Man (1970) portrays Custer
and the army as egotistical, prejudiced and ruthless, the Indians as noble and civilized. McCabe and Mrs. Miller portrays life in a frontier town as cold, squalid, greedy and uncertain. Soldier Blue (1970) also shows innocent Indians
slaughtered by soldiers. The Cowboys (1972) indicates that
boys become men when they come to terms with the necessity
for violence. The Culpepper Cattle Co. (1972) is an antidote
to all those romantic films about cattle drives, which are

shown here as mean, squalid, and dangerous. The Shootist (1976) is a very touching picture about age and approaching death, following the path cut by The Man Who Shot Liberty Vallance (1962) and Ride the High Country (1962). Buffalo Bill and the Indians, or Sitting Bull's History Lesson (1976) is even more extreme, suggesting that the entire legend of the West was a show business concoction.

Why it should have come to pass that American movies should suddenly experience a surge of examination of the United States and its past is an interesting question. The explanation certainly must take us beyond the situation in the movie industry. That the audience selects, from an enormous range of available movies, these to favor with its patronage suggests that there is a rapport. But movies here may only be catching up with the society. The middle or late sixties were an extraordinary decade of reexamination and self criticism in the United States--a country fabulous in the wealth of its critical self-examination tradition anyway. The triple-headed problems of entrenched racism, a disastrous war, and the discovery of pockets of acute poverty and near-starvation among general affluence seems to have shaken the self-confidence of a substantial body of opinion in the United States, and perhaps particularly among the college educated, who will soon be a majority of the population. The self-examination has fallen back as it were on the pieties. The pieties about patriotism and war are often invoked by the parent generation (The Green Berets did well in middle America). These are taken up and attacked in Patton (great generals are mad), M.A.S.H. (war is only bearable if you laugh) and Catch-22 (war and its makers are insane). The attitudes which college students have developed clearly come from their experiences in the family and their emotional relations with each other and these are of much concern in films of the period. There is also a sense of the intermediate generation (perhaps in their late twenties or early thirties) groping with little success for a different way of life. So the pieties of marriage and settling down are also knocked.

And yet, to the disappointment of didactic radicals, movies have not directly confronted the problems. There have been no popular films about the war in Vietnam[10], poverty among affluence, or indeed about racism. [11] There are films about these matters but they have not been big hits. They have not impacted significantly on the consciousness of the movie audience. The sixties and seventies differ in this from the thirties and forties. The depression, crime, the

war, all were directly dealt with in popular movies of the
time. Why is this no longer so, why are films nowadays usually only concerned with sociological and psychological questions? A fancy answer is not needed. Television brings the
war, poverty and race problems into every living room every
night, as they should be brought--straight. When people go
out to a movie they want something different. Is it any wonder that an audience, surfeited with the activities of student
revolutionaries on television, ignored the various attempts to
initiate a cycle of films on the subject. One may doubt whether the success of All the President's Men (1976) will usher
in a cycle of films about politics.

How do Movies and Society Interact?

We have seen in this chapter so far that movies are
related in shifting ways to what may be called a collective
consciousness of the society, to its present and immediate
concerns. This relationship is not direct and simple. Movies are sensitive to the national mood for simple reasons.
They are not created by a single individual with a camera.
They are created at all stages by a group (Gans 1957). The
idea for a movie has to strike the producer or an executive
or an agent. His or her first task is to assemble opinion
on whether or not the property is viable. Then, depending
on the filmmaker's reputation and standing, to begin exploring the question of assembling finance. Already at this stage
several dozen people may be involved. Simultaneously with
the attempt to set up finance there is the necessity of beginning to assemble talent. Often, finance will be forthcoming
only if a package of talent is arranged. Talent will, in the
first place, consist of people able to take the idea and turn
it into a script. This may be a single writer, though it
rarely is. It is never a single writer in the sense that that
writer does not constantly discuss his ideas and his progress
with the initiator--whether producer or executive--and there
are few directors who are brought in so late to the project
that they do not also take part in these discussions. If a
particularly senior or well-paid actor is involved, he may
also wish to be in on story discussions and so on. This pro-
ceeds right down the line. The writer and producer will be
discussing with the director at the time of writing the script
how things will be directed. They will perhaps not interfere
or discuss directly on the studio floor when the film is being
shot (some do, and are known as "difficult"), but with most
directors there is a good deal of interaction at that time with

the producer, with the writer, with the various actors, as
the things are worked out. Then when the film has been shot
the decisions about how it is to be cut, how it is to be scor-
ed, and how to balance the sound track, are all decisions
which are taken perhaps by one person but in consultation
with others. Thus, in film making we see society in a mi-
crocosm. The group which makes the film in a sense reflects its understanding of the subject and builds up within it
a conception of the audience it is trying to reach and adapts
the creative decisions that need to be made to that audience.
This perhaps explains why the mass media can sometimes develop an extraordinary resonance with a contemporary mood--
quite different from that ever achieved by a single creative
artist working by himself.

The structural features which produce this resonance
have been analyzed by Gans. The audience, as he points out,
is a complexly layered set of publics or subcultures. Even
the audience for such a straightforward movie as a Western
may include fans of the stars, those who like to see good
triumph over evil, those who root for the heroic individualist,
and even those who want to escape to the wide open spaces.
Somehow, this audience "follows" the creators into the studio.

To begin with, a creator is creating something for
somebody, some audience (even if only himself), which he
bears in mind. Gans calls this the audience image. This
image functions as an external observer-judge against which
to test his efforts and make his creative choices. A creator
will not have one audience image; he will develop one for each
movie and its component situations, characters and the like.
To a certain extent the creator, by trying to make a good
movie, is attempting to create an audience which corresponds
to his image for that movie. The really successful creator
knows or feels something that is shared by several publics.

Each creator has his own unique life history and tastes
which rarely correspond to those of his heterogeneous audience.
This allows him the emotional distance necessary to create
for so many divergent publics. Yet the movie making group
may be a fair cross-section of the society. Movie making
can be viewed as a decision-making process, the outcome being synthesized from the decisions each creator makes in
terms of his position in the power structure, his audience
image, and his other reference groups (peers, critics, pressure groups, superiors). This explains the insecurity so rife
in the mass media and the apparent irrationality of so many

decisions. Since the many publics are so complex, and since
success turns essentially on drawing sufficient numbers of
these into the theaters, and since each movie has to create
its own aggregate public, it is unique, and insecurity is bound
to develop. One method of trying to avoid this is the cycle,
where a successful movie is imitated in the hope of drawing
in the same public as was drawn to the movie being imitated.
All this also explains why movie making often consists of a
struggle between those with different audience images. The
rewards come only to those who guess right and, since so
much is at stake, each person fights for the victory of his
own image.

Movie making, then, resembles committee work. One
might say: movies are a committee creation. There may be
a powerful chairman and secretary, but the total group con-
tributes in terms of audience images. All the notions of group
dynamics can be applied. Movie making is risky, and groups
tend to take less risk than individuals (they try to make movies to please as many as possible). Some individuals dominate even though they are not highest in formal status. The
past record of an individual may carry much weight even with
those whose initial inclination was another way. The principal feedback is of course box-office receipts. Curiously, before a film is released there is a great deal of direct observation of preview audiences and their reaction to the film.
Changes are made as a result. (Ross 1950, Dunne 1969).
Afterwards, one can understand lack of attention to flops (they've
done all they can and now want to get on to new things), but
what of the lack of close observation and analysis of successes? So far as I know most explanations of the success of
Bonnie and Clyde, Easy Rider, The Graduate, Woodstock,
Love Story, Airport, The Godfather, The Sting, The Exorcist,
Jaws, are the sheerest speculation about what are, after all,
very different films. This relates back to my earlier admis-
sion that success is difficult to explain. All the more reason, one would think, to attempt the job. It's pretty clear
that different films draw in different audiences. It's also
pretty clear that the different audiences respond to the films
they enjoy in different ways. Those who smoked pot in the
last 20 minutes of 2001 (a space odyssey of creation and re-
birth) were rather different from those who hummed their way
through The Sound of Music (goodness shines out). Or were
they? No one knows.

Gans himself has not carefully explained the concepts
which underlie his theory of subcultures. The idea that people

enjoy films that mirror their aspirations or problems is as confining as the idea that they enjoy films as vicarious experience or as escape. Let us look more closely at the audience side of the movies and society relationship.

NOTES

1. J. P. Mayer, in the "Retrospect" of the Arno Press reprint of his 1946 classic Sociology of Film, argues that there is a contradiction between admitting that movies influence fashions, hair-styles, courting, etc., and being sceptical of their ability to cause juvenile delinquency and other serious effects. However, others, including myself, see no contradiction. No one denies that movies have an obvious influence on superficial matters. The debate is entirely about whether movies have any deep influence on the core values and behavior, whether they can alone warp a person or a whole society.

2. They no longer do because movies are no longer a majority but rather a minority pastime. Similarly, the market for films is more difficult which, curiously, makes the industry less vulnerable to self-appointed censors. See Chapter III.

3. For example, different radio stations and different magazines and newspapers appeal to very different groups; downtown theaters, suburban shopping center theaters, and drive-ins are also different markets.

4. By and large this book sticks to contemporary movies. But a good case can be made that this process happened before. As outlined in Chapter III, the post-World-War-II audience was very different from what it had been. We see in that period too the positive feedback of social changes in movies. Were not short skirts, "flapper" behavior, smoking and drinking immensely aided and abetted by the "influence" (albeit superficial) of movies? And did not movies, in pursuit of the "fast" audience--and perhaps forgetful in the "fast" society of Hollywood, California, of the forces ranged against "fastness," "modernity," urbanism, booze, etc.--go "too far" in some of their themes and call forth the negative feedback of censorship and control?

5. There is a very funny article by Robert Marcus (1970) in which he argues that the whole film is about homo-

sexual, not adulterous, impulses.

6.   Misogyny should not be confused with homosexuality.   Among other things, homosexuals as a rule do not dislike women.   One might equally well interpret the hostility
to women as stemming from their use of sex as bait to the
marriage trap.   To get sex the men have to marry.   Had
they entered into it for other and better reasons the sex
might be better, the misogyny less.

7.   Andrew Carnegie, the millionaire, was the author
of the best-selling bible of success, The Empire of Business
(1917).   Cf.   Dale Carnegie (1936); which in itself was a revival of Samuel Smiles' Self Help (1862).

8.   Thus unintentionally collaborating with the gangsters they abhorred who thrived only because "vice" was illegal.

9.   I must thank Robert Macmillan for making me
completely rethink, and redraft, the above few paragraphs.

10.   Since this was written, I have read Julian Smith's
book, Looking Away (1975), in which he argues cogently that
American films were constantly trying to come to terms with
the Vietnam war and its effects.   Smith's book is based on
close examination of the films, and provides fascinating con-
firmation of the thesis of this book that American movies are
always intensely close to and critical of American social developments.

11.   Since Roots, it is clear that television has appro-
priated this issue.   See Chapter V.

III

THE DIVERSE AUDIENCES
AND FUNCTIONS OF MOVIES

Film is a phenomenon in society. Films are many
and diverse, but they can be classed together in different
ways for different purposes: by country, by period, by director, writer, star, by production company, by producer,
by general type (comedy, romance, drama, musical, adventure, war, Western, skin-flick, etc.), and by specialized type
(e.g., spy-spoof, psychological Western, bikini beach comedies). The people who make up the audience are equally
many and diverse, but they too can be classed together in
various ways in order to yield what might be called audience
subcultures. They can be classed by age, sex, nationality,
ethnic group, religion, education, social class, occupation,
income, marital status, part of the country, nearness to town,
leisure habits, etc. As movies can require combined classifications (e.g., comedy-Western), or also overlap several
without quite falling into any, so too do people fall under different classifications at different times.

Herbert J. Gans has argued (1974) that certain types
of films attract particular classifications of people, and these
he calls "taste subcultures." Examples are the liking blue-
collar males have for fast-moving action movies,[1] the liking
females have for romances, the liking children have for animal adventure stories. Puzzling over the popularity of A-
merican films and television shows with the British working
class (1959), Gans concluded that they dealt with themes--
egalitarianism and upward social mobility--relatively neglected in British movies despite the fascination of these themes
for that class.

The importance of Gans's ideas is that they are the
first breakthrough in the social psychology of taste. Hither-
tofore, taste was a mysterious matter: preferences for one
movie over another just developed inexplicably. The audience
was a great mystery, a black box. Once we have discovered

patterns of taste preference, they can serve greatly to illuminate movies as a social phenomenon and help show how, and to what extent, they affect their audience. Clearly, Gans' premise is that people want to see their preoccupations illustrated and dramatized: social mobility, romance, adventure. Clearly, also, this is pretty simple-minded. Others have suggested the audience wishes to escape its preoccupations (although, arguably, dramas of upward mobility may be escape fantasies); others, that audiences want to play; still others that they want to learn. In this chapter we shall ask what functions movies perform for their audiences, and whether they perform different functions for different taste subcultures. Our answer will have to be that they perform many functions, and that these may be combined and recombined in the same individual on different occasions, and for different groups on the same occasion. Our explanation will not lead us to predict that a certain kind of film will be popular with a certain kind of audience. There remains an element of uncertainty, of creativity--an imponderable element such as the mood of the society or of the taste subculture--that makes prediction hazardous.

In Chapter II we saw how Hollywood, cushioned by high profits until television appeared, was able to treat its never really homogeneous audience as though it were. Hollywood films were pitched towards the lowest common denominator, or so it was said, and all the divisions of class, education, religion, and race in America were ignored. As long as it was profitable, this policy was unlikely to be challenged, especially as Hollywood films were also exported with a good deal of success. Either Hollywood was providing what audiences almost everywhere wanted or audiences almost everywhere were happy to take whatever Hollywood offered. That the second of these two possibilities is least likely became clear in the early fifties when television began to challenge movies for their place as the preeminent family entertainment. Had it been the case that worldwide audiences were being forced to take whatever Hollywood offered, American material would have had a far harder time establishing its ascendency. Its cheapness and availability do not suffice to explain why American material comes off best with television audiences almost anywhere in the world where it is in free competition with the local product.

We have also seen how, when facing the economic challenge of television, Hollywood was so uncertain that it was providing what the public wanted that it concluded that it should switch to making films on a lavish scale that television would be unable to imitate. Stars, color, spectacle, the great outdoors, the wide screen--these were exploited to the hilt. Films became bigger, as well as longer; modestly budgeted pictures and "B" grade second features virtually disappeared. Yet, despite all this, crises recurred. Hollywood was beset with problems which forced drastic structural change. Studios sold off their fixed assets. Stars broke free from their exclusive contracts. Independent producers were more and more looked-to for new ideas. More than ever Hollywood became gimmick- and cycle-conscious. If a new kind of film made a hit, every company tried to produce copies and follow-ups. The Elvis Presley films, the bikini beach films, the motorcycle gang films, the American International and Hammer horror films, the cycle of films about bizarre psychopaths triggered by Psycho, the spy cycle which began with the James Bond films, the rush to film Broadway musicals, the cycle of Indians-good, whiteman-bad Westerns, the violent yet comic gangster cycle beginning with Bonnie and Clyde, the ill-fated student revolution cycle, the cycle of police detective adventures and the subject of our own case study, the cycle about the travails of married life.

What we see going on here is a search for what will please, what will bring back, the lost audience. Nothing will do that, of course, and what happens instead is that these films are reaching out to the fragments of the former audience. The audience was never homogeneous in taste and outlook, any more than America was ever a homogeneous society. The appearance of homogeneity was a by-product of the fact that, in attending Hollywood films, people found a common meeting ground. But once competition arrived that meeting ground became television, and either a special reason or a special position in society was required before people would get themselves organized to go out to the movies. No longer was a habit or a star sufficient reason to be forking out money at the box office. No longer were there paying customers who displayed virtually no interest in what was being shown inside. Only if what they knew (or thought they knew) that was showing inside was to their taste would they pay up. No longer a black box, this newly structured audience has revealed a lot about itself. It is less provincial and less complacent than its predecessor. It gets many different sorts of things out of movies (but perhaps audiences always did). The sense in which movies are an escape for this audience is subtle and easily misunderstood. To understand the diversity of movie functions we need to look at how the parochial American movie culture has broken down, partly on account of external influence.

The Decline of Provincialism

That America was never a homogeneous society, I take for granted. But another factor was at work which it is more difficult to disentangle. We might call this the end of American provincialism. [2] That the United States has for much of its existence been a self-regarding and rather parochial culture hardly needs arguing. Practically any description of America published by a foreign traveler before 1950 will attest to it. Doubtless connected with the past revolutionary break from Europe and her wicked ways, this cultural outlook made America the home of the "hayseed." Two world wars and the transport revolution were needed before this isolation (so strongly encapsulated in the policies of isolationism and America-first-ism) began to be broken down. American self-sufficiency, insularity, if you like, is reflected in the films of the great days of Hollywood. American society and culture seem to have, and to need, no reference point outside themselves, no aspirations other than more of the same. None of this would be true of America in general today, although it is still true of much of the country. The gradual breakdown of this provincialism coincided with or perhaps even was contributed to by the drastic changes in Hollywood that we have been describing. To explain and tie all this together, let us take a look at the development of Hollywood and its provincialism.

In the silent period, of course, movies were international. The stars might not be well known, but the splicing-in of a few titles in the local language was sufficient to turn a film from any country into an entertainment for Americans. With the advent of sound, and the prior development, not only of the star system, but of Hollywood's monopolistic tendencies, the import of foreign films into the American market dwindled to a trickle. Dubbing was a crude and unsatisfactory device, subtitles were unsightly and often difficult to see. British films with their rapid and clipped speech in unfamiliar accents often left American audiences baffled. When foreign talent in writing, direction or performance looked promising the answer was: buy it and bring it to Hollywood. From the twenties onwards Hollywood was a huge vortex in world cinema, sucking into its center talent from every film industry in the world, even the Russian. [3]

It must be remembered that in its early years the American cinema was regarded as bold and experimental. Griffith, von Stroheim and Chaplin were revered by filmmakers throughout the world as innovative creators. The freedom they enjoyed seems to have dwindled during the twenties, as the industry became bigger and somewhat more conservative. But new talent was imported such as Sjöström (Sweden), Wilder, (Germany), Ophuls (Austria), Hitchcock (Britain), Wyler (Switzerland), and Lubitsch (Germany). Nevertheless, many observers maintained that the truly experimental and exciting cinema was by then being created mostly elsewhere than in Hollywood: in the twenties in Russia and Germany; in the thirties in France; in the forties in Italy; in the fifties in Japan and France again; and so on. Hollywood, meanwhile, had "gone commercial" and stifled creative freedom. [4] Such an account is completely superficial.

The cruel fact is, however, that much of this foreign experimental effort failed to pay off at the box office, either in the country concerned, or abroad. Meanwhile, Hollywood picked off such persons of talent as caught its eye, or could be tempted away, and set them to making entertaining pictures in the California sunshine. This recruiting reached its peak in the forties, when a positive flood of refugees from Europe came into the American cinema. Some of the great "black cinema" (doom-laden melodrama) of the forties was created by refugees; Curtiz, Lang, Siodmak. Fine, if sometimes gloomy entertainment resulted, it is true, but in-bred and self-preoccupied to a fault. One sees this self-regard everywhere: the cozy provincialism of Meet Me in St. Louis (when all is right with Middle America all is right with the world), made by an American, Minnelli, is matched by the adoring portrait of small-town life made by an immigrant, Hitchcock, in Shadow of a Doubt (friendly Uncle Charlie is really a killer). The Hungarian Michael Curtiz's filming of James M. Cain's very American story of avarice and ambition in California, Mildred Pierce (self-made tycoon Joan Crawford finds that money interferes with her relationships with men, and ruins her relationship with her daughter). Even in the exotic setting of Casablanca (disillusioned with love and liberalism, Humphrey Bogart revives his faith with self-sacrifice), Curtiz's people behave like characters in a thirties American movie, not like the sophisticated cosmopolitans they are supposed to be. Never mind, all of this made splendid movies. True, but the last real experiment in the American cinema, before the gimmick craze of the fifties, was Welles' Citizen Kane in 1940 (the rise and fall

of Charles Foster Kane, newspaper tycoon). While the film
was not a flop, Welles did not prove a bonanza; he was never
to get freedom in Hollywood again. [5]

After the war, new and exciting cinematic innovation
came again from Europe. In Italy, Rossellini and De Sica
pioneered a style quickly dubbed "neo-realism" in reaction
to the glossy, pseudo-Hollywood, "white telephone" films
(featuring artificial characters who used white telephones)
that were standard Italian fare. Undoubtedly influenced by
the documentary style, these films concentrated on the grit-
tiness of the ordinary and the everyday, and often used amateur actors. Rossellini's Rome, Open City (1946), De Sica's
Shoeshine (1946), Bicycle Thief (1948) and Umberto D (1952),
Visconti's L'Ossessione (1942) and La Terra trema (1948) were
about partisans, poverty, old age, unemployment, peasants.
Rome, Open City, chronicled the hideous struggle that went
on in Rome as the Germans withdrew, and before the allies
had entered the city. Shoeshine portrayed the lives of the
shoeshine boys in Rome after the war. Bicycle Thief is a-
bout one of the army of unemployed in Milan after the war
who gets a job, but the bicycle he needs to get to work is
stolen. So he rather ineptly tries to steal one, is pursued,
and ends up with nothing. Umberto D (roughly equivalent to
John Doe) is a mood piece about the pathos and humiliation
of being old and poor. Ossessione is an Italian version of
the novel, The Postman Always Rings Twice by James M.
Cain, in which a woman tempts a man into crime. La Terra
trema is another mood piece about the harsh lives and nar-
rowly confining society of Sicilian fishermen. Shot largely
on location, these films strove to capture the precise texture
of life as it is experienced. Perhaps these films and the
British documentary films of the thirties indirectly influenced
Hollywood's brief phase of semi-documentary crime films of
the late forties, produced by Mark Hellinger, Louis de Roch-
emont and others. Examples are The House on 92nd Street
(1945), a story of Second World War espionage shot largely
at or near where it all actually happened; and The Naked City
(1948), where the investigation of a crime is used as an excuse to explore the slummier districts of New York City. A
more obvious pair of influences are the "March of Time" documentaries about the war, and the news reporting on radio
and film.

Neo-realism fizzled out in Italy in the fifties and by
the end of that decade filmic excitement was being stirred up
in France by the New Wave of young critics turned filmmak-

ers. Vadim, Truffaut, Godard, Chabrol, Malle and many
others, first came to prominence then. Their style too was
a revolt against the established directors of France. But
there was no real school here, no striving for a unity of outlook. What there was was a group of talented young individuals coming to the forefront at about the same moment.

Just before the New Wave made headlines, changes
were fomenting in Britain in the novel and the drama. What
became known as the Angry Young Man movement (Allsop
1958), similarly comprised a group of disparate but undoubtedly talented young men who came to the forefront close together. Kingsley Amis and John Wain in the novel; John
Osborne, Arnold Wesker, N. F. Simpson, Harold Pinter in
the drama (Taylor 1962); Tony Richardson and Lindsay Anderson the interpreters. It was not long before all this spil-
led over into the making of films. The best-known are the
following. Look Back in Anger (1958)--Jimmy Porter, educated out of his class by the welfare state, married to a middle-class girl, is filled with frustration and rage because he
makes his living running a stall in a market. The Entertainer (1960) is Archie Rice, failed and tired musichall comedian,
given to dreams of success and the odd seduction. Room at
the Top (1959) is there for ambitious and calculating working-
class northerner Joe Lambton, who is prepared to dump the
woman who really loves him and whom he lives, for the rewards of the boss's daughter and a position in the family
firm. Saturday Night and Sunday Morning (1960) shows us
a northern working-class lad who gets his kicks out of secret
sexual adventure with other people's wives, and who eventually meets his match in a girl whom he will end up marrying,
but who defiantly throws stones at the housing subdivision
where they will probably live. A Kind of Loving (1962) is
the sexual kind, used by an ordinary girl to get her man to
marry her. His struggle to break free from her mother,
•and give the shotgun marriage a chance, provides the rest
of the story. A Taste of Honey (1962) is about a warm-
hearted girl who goes to bed with a black sailor, gets pregnant and is befriended by an equally lonely and forlorn homo-
sexual. As a group, these and many other films were lumped together and labeled the new "kitchen-sink realist" school.
It is curious that this creative surge was extremely parochial,
because it was the vanguard of the British invasion of the A-
merican cinema market. By parochial, I refer to the fact
that these films were concerned with very British matters.
The hero of John Osborne's Look Back in Anger is an em-
bittered working-class youth who has received a state subsi-

dized university education, which has left him ill-suited for anything but extremely observant and articulate. Most of the other films have working-class heroes, usually with thick proletarian accents. Yet it was from this newly discovered lower-class vitality that Britain's great international cultural influence (1963-1968) was to come in film, music, fashion and life style. A crucial movie was the bawdy Tom Jones (1963), set in the eighteenth century, but made by the Angry Young Men and reflecting their new outlook. It was a breakthrough from the image of the British as dull, uptight, and frigid, epitomized in the unconsummated union and the repressed passion of Brief Encounter (1946). In Tom Jones the British come over as fun-loving, roguish and raunchy. The film did extremely well in America and its profits financed other, less commercial, experiments.

As we have remarked, the American movie audience was not thitherto amenable to the foreign product. In the forties the British company J. Arthur Rank had almost gone bankrupt by making lavish films which on that account they naively thought would be popular in the American market (e.g., Caesar and Cleopatra 1945, Scott of the Antarctic 1948, The Bad Lord Byron 1948). Yet by the mid-sixties all this had changed. Resistance was over. British films, like almost everything British, were suddenly in vogue in America. Especially remarkable were A Hard Day's Night (1964) ostensibly a documentary about a pop group on tour, starring the Beatles but directed by an American (Richard Lester); and Blow-Up (1966), which captured the essence of "swinging London" through the adventures of a photographer who thinks he has observed a murder. Oddly, this film was directed and written by an Italian (Michelangelo Antonioni). It was also in the sixties that foreign language films first made a great splash, such as The Seventh Seal (Death can be cheated), La Dolce vita (24 hours in the life of a jaded journalist in Rome), Hercules (H. helps Jason succeed to the throne), A Man and a Woman (young widow meets young widower, romance blooms), Elvira Madigan (army officer runs off with

---

Opposite: In Britain it was stage drama that got ahead of society in general in the fifties. The vanguard of this "Angry" drama was John Osborne's Look Back in Anger. Brought to the screen by Warner Brothers in 1958, it was directed by Tony Richardson, and starred Mary Ure, Gary Raymond (center) and Richard Burton (as Jimmy Porter). Porter is an educated son of the working class, who is fascinated by and enraged at the middle class.

Premarital sex among the British working class (June Ritchie) and Alan Bates): the man keeps his clothes on. Such a scene was pretty daring, at the time (1962). Directing A Kind of Loving for the Rank Organization, from a screenplay by Keith Waterhouse and Willis Hall (based on Stan Barstow's novel), was John Schlesinger. Schlesinger has gone on to further explore sexual themes in Darling (1964), which deals with promiscuity, and Midnight Cowboy (1969) and the remarkable Sunday, Bloody Sunday (1971) both of which deal with homosexuality.

circus girl--they enter a suicide pact when his money runs
out--set to Mozart), Clint Eastwood's Italian Westerns.

The point to be made here is that three factors allowed these dents to be made in parochialism. One, the easiest
to grasp, is changes in the American film industry. The second is the new saleability of foreign movies, and American
interest in investing in them (Guback 1969). The third, harder to pin down, is changes in the entire cultural mood of
America. Industrial change was brought on by television and
a successful federal antitrust suit against the movie companies. Drastic structural change was forced on the movie industry. Vertical integration was dismantled. Block booking
declined. Independent production flourished. The total audience shrank, as did the number of movie theaters. Increasingly the companies resorted to "runaway" productions--shoot-
ing American films abroad where costs were lower. The A-
merican movie market, then, disorganized and declining, was
ripe for foreign intrusion--although, typically, it was American businessmen who were to take the initiative.

The factor allowing these dents to be made in the film
industry was the increasing number of foreign films in which
American money was invested. At first foreign earnings were
used to finance American pictures shot in Europe. [6] Later
on, local branches of American companies backed entirely local films, and especially those which showed some promise
of being popular in the United States.

It is difficult to be precise about changes in the cultural outlook of the United States. Roughly, it seems as
though the early sixties saw a repudiation of the melting pot
mentality, of the attempt to gloss over or ignore the vast
differences between Americans (Glazer and Moynihan 1963).
The way was led, I believe, by youth and the blacks. Youth
was fighting for a cultural freedom and identity of its own
(see Jarvie 1972, chapter 3). The blacks, in the course of
a struggle for civil rights, came to develop a new consciousness of themselves as different as well as equal. This height-
ened ethnic consciousness. Later subculture identities af-
firmed were Chicano, hard-hats, middle-Americans, and so
on, in addition to the traditional ones like Jews, WASP, Italo-
Americans, Puerto Ricans, and Chinese. Bold affirmation
and approval of ethnic and subcultural diversity was a crucial
break with the past, when the ideology of the melting pot was
that such differences should be submerged in a newly acquired
American identity. This break also revealed a diversified

audience for movies, less provincial and decidedly complex.

We have already mentioned television's impact upon the industry. It was a double-barreled threat, because America's loss of cultural parochialism might partly also be attributed to television. Just as the countryside was given the same television fare as the cities, so American televiewers were fed a lot of material from abroad (although one wonders why familiarity with and curiosity about the world had not been achieved by the mass circulation magazines Time and Newsweek years before). It is difficult to avoid the thought that profound changes were taking place in the American consciousness as the memory of the war faded, the reality of the cold war diminished, affluence and leisure increased, and higher education became more widespread. The idea that American experience was unique and complete, that the United States could solve all its own problems without external reference, was underminded. This in turn may have had something to do with the long-term effects of America's assumption of world leadership, and the consequent necessity of turning outwards.

The full social and political explanation for these cultural changes is for other scholars to work out. What it meant for the movies was that they were confronted with a very different market--or markets. Smaller, better defined, more open-minded towards foreign films and mores.

Anyway, to tie all this together: what I am suggesting is that a complex of factors was at work in America which had the result of fragmenting a homogeneous and insular American audience. Whereas in the fifties French, Italian and British attempts to get widespread distribution for their national product had failed, by the sixties American companies were importing, selling and profiting from the foreign product. American movies, as a result, entered a different market. They were also, as we shall see, an altered social phenomenon.

The first selling point for foreign movies was undoubtedly sex. Long before the American cinema had dared to exploit sex, Roger Vadim was promoting Brigitte Bardot in And God Created Woman (sexy slut marries one brother and sleeps with another, 1957), as the first foreign sex superstar. British sex came later. The crucial breakthrough beyond the urban audience for foreign sex films was undoubtedly the Beatles, a phenomenon we must simply take for granted here. The

Beatles took the creative center of pop music across the Atlantic to Britain where it remained for a year or two. Their films, A Hard Day's Night (1964) and Help! (1965), were a great success. London became a sort of swinging mecca towards which American youth looked as the miniskirt was invented, as pop singers and photographers seemed to dominate the lifestyle, and as films glamorizing the whole business were churned out. The success of the lustily sexual Tom Jones was crucial in overthrowing many misconceptions. This awareness of foreign customs and sexuality, this willingness to admire a foreign lifestyle, was something new in America, and surely independent of whatever particular crises were afflicting the American film industry.

That this cultural transformation was taking place just as the American film industry was shuddering through the latest of its many crises was lucky for America and that industry. Since the immediate post-war crisis (1946-1947) the American movie industry had been shrinking as its audience shrank. In addition to shrinking, its audience could increasingly easily be subdivided into clearly identifiable subaudiences, primarily defined by age, but also by income, education and ethnic background. It was less and less feasible to program a theater in a university town in exactly the same way as one in a factory town. What would be successful in New York or Los Angeles was not necessarily going to bring them in in the boondocks--although it must not be forgotten that one side effect of television was to close the gap between New York and the boondocks more than was thought possible at an earlier time.

Some theaters, then, remained open despite television, and this meant that either an irreducible minimum of films had to be found to be shown, or habits such as programming each film for only one week had to change. To get enough films, imports could be resorted to. When a hit developed it could be run for a long time, then reissued six months or a year later to draw in everyone who was fed up with hearing about the film but had missed it first time round. Both strategies have become standard.

The audience for sexy pictures was perhaps the thin end of the wedge, for their favorites sometimes overlapped with the tastes of the art-house audience. And God Created Woman (the sexually aggressive woman exists and BB is her name), La Dolce vita (the sweet life is a bore), Never on Sunday (happiness is being a Greek prostitute, 1960) Hiro-

shima, mon amour (sex between a female collaborator and
a Japanese from Hiroshima fuses memory, guilt and expiation,
1960) could be sold to both. Other enterprising businessmen
imported cheap Italian spectaculars featuring muscle-builders
as heroes. These made phenomenal returns. And then came
the influx of British films. Italian (or "spaghetti") Westerns
were another profitable item. The Westerns, and the British
films, which included a lot of gory remakes of classic Hollywood horror pictures caught on with the young audience, a
group that was beginning to define itself very aggressively
during the sixties. The youth market was something of which
manufacturing and retail industry had long been aware. In
the sixties it changed rapidly. Before then it had been catered to by films featuring rock-and-roll groups, surfing or
other beach romps, horror and motorcycling. Very suddenly,
during the sixties, this audience grew up. People of high
school and college age developed much more sophisticated
tastes: to some extent for foreign films, to some extent for
more sophisticated American films. One can see this beginning with The Graduate (what is there to do after graduation?)
and Bonnie and Clyde (the sexy but rather inept bank robber
as hero; the bad and the beautiful), both of which were sophisticated pieces of technical movie making, and also about
quite atypical characters.

All of this had much to do, as I have hinted, with
transformations which were going on in American society in
the sixties. One might generalize and say that the mood of
the forties was largely caught up with fighting a major war
and then recovering from it. The fifties are to the outside
observer a curious decade in the United States--one of apparent political tranquility and social quietism, yet possessed
it would seem by the frightful malaise of McCarthyism and
its aftermath. The communications media were scrutinized
closely during the McCarthy period--Hollywood being twice
investigated, once in 1947 and again in 1950-1951 (Kanfer
1973). One result was that the movie industry became politically rather cautious and some of the more radically-mind-
ed filmmakers either left in disgust or were pushed out of
the industry. Although McCarthyism was eventually stopped,
the damage was done. Hollywood was already demoralized
by its economic crisis; this cat among the pigeons of its creators crushed the spirit of experiment and change which under normal circumstances would have survived. The unevent-
fulness of fifties' movies may have had something to do with
the rigidity of the industry and·its difficulties in responding
to the challenge to regain its audience from television. Per-

haps as a pendulum reaction to the social and political image
of the fifties as complacent, we find in the sixties a repudiation of much that the fifties stood for; a rediscovery of rad-
icalism and perhaps the suggestion that it can be respectable,
even American to be radical; a general loosening up of the
society, a questioning of sacred cows, the beginnings of social and political rethinking and experimenting. Much later
we find these changes reflected in Hollywood in the movie
industry. In fact we find the ridiculous spectacle (as in the
hippie executives and directors portrayed in Alex in Wonder-
land, 1970, which Paul Mazursky directed from a script he
wrote with Larry Tucker) of Hollywood people wheezing and
puffing after the youth audience.

America is an enormously large and diversified society
and many of its reactions are unpredictable--as movie companies find out when they gamble that this or that film will
be a success or will flop. The industry certainly never expected that M. A. S. H. (a black comedy about Army surgeons),
would be a great success and they were awfully worried a-
bout Woodstock (four hours of the biggest rock concert ever
held) too. Yet both found an audience. One would think that
rational investors would insist that sooner or later the industry get to know its audience on a somewhat better basis than
simply throwing out a whole lot of movies each year and hop-
ing that some of them will catch on. This method is quite
rational in the production of popular music singles because
each one represents a small investment. But even an inexpensive movie like Easy Rider represents an "up front" investment of $600,000. It may be that sort of sum will soon
bespeak a rather high budget, given the risks involved. As
long ago as 1965, A. H. Howe (1965) (in charge of investment in motion pictures for the First National Bank in Los
Angeles) said that in devising security for a loan to movie
makers the finished movie was always given the book value
of zero. Even in 1965, the risk with any completed movie
was so great that sober bankers had to value an untried product of that kind at zero. In a 1971 updating of the article,
Howe's position was the same.

The miracle is perhaps that movies go on being made.
Ticket prices have gone up, but total revenues have fallen.
But when success is achieved the rewards are so large that
the continued survival of the movie industry is perhaps less
of a miracle than at first it seems. As Fletcher Knebel
points out in Look (1970), while only one movie in seven
makes money, the money to be made is better than ever.

Why else would money flow in from oilmen, real estate, toy manufacturers, and so on? He also points out that quite a few films obviously not aimed at the youth market bulk very large in the year-end box-office figures. His examples are The Sound of Music (an Austrian family becomes a singing sensation and escapes from the Nazis to America); Funny Girl (a music hall star loves a gambler and ne'er-do-well); Airport (many dramatic events occur to different people when their lives cross during a blizzard at an airport); Beyond the Valley of the Dolls (adventures of a three-girl pop-group in Hollywood with narcotics, pills, sex and mass murder); The Love Bug (an odd car brings a racing driver luck). Doubtless Hotel (many dramatic events occur to different people when their lives cross in a major hotel); The Love Machine (television executive with great sexual capacity turns his back on it all); and Airport 75 (a disabled jumbo jet is somehow safely landed) confirm that this is still true.

How does all the above discussion bear on the social psychology of the movies, on films as a social phenomenon? The connections are easy to draw. Once upon a time movies loomed large as a social phenomenon to a rather parochial, isolated and poorly differentiated American audience. Inexorable forces have changed the audience, widened the kinds of films available to it, and, of most concern to us here, altered the social psychological processes at work on this social phenomenon. The two mechanisms I would select are those of the two-step (or multi-step) flow of communications; and the differentiation of taste subcultures. Gans has argued persuasively in several places (e.g., 1966, 1974) that the audience for motion pictures, as for other media, can be said to cluster into certain subcultural groups, defined by age, class, wealth, education, ethnicity, urban or rural locations, and the like. These subcultures crystallize into taste patterns for certain kinds of material on radio and television, in newspapers, magazines and other reading matter, and for movies, and within these for certain kinds of stories and content. In particular, for example, working-class audiences are quite intrigued by stories which reflect their own aspirations to upward-mobility. They are quite scathing when middle-class views of the police are presented in films.

Fully to grasp how such an amorphous group as a taste subculture can be treated as a subaudience which is worth catering to, we must add the Katz-Lazarsfeld (1955) ideas. In an elaborate study of personal influence, Katz and Lazarsfeld were concerned with understanding the role

of opinion leaders in the formation of taste and preference
in the mass media. To recapitulate: they discovered that
people in a neighborhood, or at school or at college or at
work, grouped themselves into small clusters which tended
to take their leadership in matters of movie taste from an
opinion leader--someone who took a greater interest in the
medium than the others and who was therefore looked to for
guidance by them. While the opinion leader did not dictate
taste, he (often she) was a reference point, a place to begin,
and seemed to exert considerable influence. Hence the theory
of the two-step flow of communications. Messages got through
to a group not by reaching each individual directly, but by
first being received by the opinion leader, who then relays
it to the group which accepts her influence. Later research
has multiplied the number of steps as the taste subcultures
have become more complex.

Once we grasp all this, we see how important the
diversification of the audience is to the movie maker. A
better understanding of the social psychology of movies leads
to different assumptions. It indicates first of all that word
of mouth rather than direct advertisement is the primary
factor making for audience interest and hence for success.
It means second of all that individual movies can no longer
be expected to appeal equally across all social divisions.
It follows that modest budgeting and the tailoring of content
to suit certain taste subcultures is a prudent production strategy. This does not mean that all-seeing moguls will tell
creators what to do. On the contrary, it implies that shrewd
moguls will try to have stables of creators who have or appear to have rapport with certain taste subcultures. The
moguls will then, within tight budgetary limits, give these
creators their heads. Those that persistently fail to pull it
off will not have spent too much money, and those that do
pull it off can be expected every so often to make a bonanza.
Knebel relates a case in point. Warner Brothers put up
$100,000 for the shooting of Woodstock, and, presented with
the footage, invested another $900,000 in an elaborate edit-
ing job by movie-freak kids. After a bit of hesitation (was
it too long?) they spent another $1,000,000 to buy musical
rights. Total investment was a modest two million. Returns
were not final when Knebel wrote, but they were very substantial. Woodstock may not have outgrossed Airport, but
the profits on it were sufficient to ensure that if Hollywood
did not finance further films by its makers, someone else
would. Woodstock itself was an imitation of Monterey Pop
(1969), which in turn was an imitation of Jazz on a Summer's

Day (1960). Woodstock, then, was not a new idea, just a successful reuse of an old idea. It in turn has been imitated profitably by Gimme Shelter (1970) and Concert for Bangladesh (1972).

How Do Movies Function for Their Audience?

Our exploration of Gans' ideas is not complete once the two-step flow theory and taste subcultures are combined. Movies, I believe, offer a multiplicity of satisfactions to their audiences, function for them in a host of ways. Any too straightforward linking of taste subculture with a type of film runs into this problem. Let us now examine the matter.

The commonest way of explaining why an audience is satisfied by a film is to talk of identification and escape, this might be called the explanation from popular (or folk) social psychology. Movies are said to picture either heroes or events or locales with which the moviegoer can identify. To identify with a virile or successful hero, to feel part of the exciting events which surround him, to imagine oneself transplanted to exotic locales, is a form of vicarious enjoyment. The moviegoer is thought to plunge himself or herself into the fantasy life of the movie in order to escape the oppressions of his present concerns.

One reason for the widespread popularity of the identification-escape theory is simply its plausibility. Anyone who has studied the infrared photographs of the audiences at children's matinees, and seen the rapt--one is tempted to say "transported"--expressions on the children's faces; anyone who has been in an audience cheering on the hero of an action film; anyone who has seen people guiltily dabbing their eyes when the lights went up after a "weepy"; any of these will say that people at movies get, as we way, "carried away." But is this phenomenon any different from that of two people in a bus engrossed in conversation who thereby miss their stop; or from someone's concentrating on a piece of reading so that nothing distracts him? As far as I can see, a gripping novel that one cannot put down; a compelling piece of argument that one must see through to the end; and so on, are no different. The only reason that is ever offered as to why getting carried away by a movie is any different, is that movies are visual. This in itself is out of date, since music and talk have for long been integral parts of the grip of many

movies, e.g. Psycho (vicious knife murders happen in an old
house). One must I suppose introspect a bit. The dramatic
media may involve a person more, overwhelm one more, but
I would contend that these are quantitative differences, not
qualitative ones.

Harold Mendelsohn (1966) argues that identification-escape analysis is simultaneously naive and fruitless. Such a-
nalysis suggests how movies function on the basis of the scant-
iest (if any) knowledge of what goes on in people's life space.
He notes that very little is understood of the nature of audience gratification in the mass media. To put it a little differently, what we do know does not support identification and
escape as the only or even the chief function of movies. Take
a case in point. One can certainly see in many of the popular
films of the late sixties and early seventies such as M. A. S. H.
Easy Rider, Midnight Cowboy, Five Easy Pieces and so
on, certain recurring themes. M. A. S. H. features a pair
of expert surgeons kidding authority but performing essential
work in saving wounded soldiers just behind the Korean war
front. Easy Rider features a pair of hippie motorcycle bums
who travel aimlessly across the Southwest on the profits of
a big heroin deal. Midnight Cowboy shows how a symbiotic
relationship develops between a consumptive cripple and a
Texas stud, both trying to survive on their wits in New York
City. Five Easy Pieces explains its hero's restless wander-
ing and aimlessness as a reaction to the cloying home atmosphere of talented and ambitious musicians. Seeing through it,
and also through himself, he cuts himself adrift in society.

Perhaps the most obvious common theme is that the
central characters are alienated from their social surroundings. The standard life goals of our society such as education, a job, a girl (a boy), a family, wealth and success, a
home, a vacation, are either matters of sheer indifference
or are entirely taken for granted and dissatisfaction remains.
In the films about marriage discussed in Chapter II, none of
the couples is facing problems of any great magnitude to do
with career, money, or standing in society. At best these
are minor matters. The temptation to see significance in
all this alienation and introspection is very strong, especially
as the movies mentioned have been successful despite having
no established stars in them--indeed they have created new
stars whose appeal lies less in their glamor than in their
anti-heroic parts and their unpretentious off-screen lifestyle.
Has their popularity anything to do with whether members of
an audience approve of figures who portray and act out their

own idealized self images? Too little is known for more
than tentative answers, but the problem demands explanation.
And whatever conclusion we come to, no simplistic doctrine
of identification and escape is going to work. Many of these
films look more like reflections upon the condition of alienation, a condition in which their audiences are interested because they are experiencing it themselves, or they know others
who are. It is interesting that none of these films "solves"
the alienation. Zabriskie Point (student rebel meets liberated
girl) ends with an explosion, a meaningless gesture that may
be fantasy. James Bond and other spy heroes exploit their
own alienation for fun and excitement. This may function as
escape.

The decisive empirical argument against the idea that
the function of movies is escape is the simple fact that people
whose lives are not apparently dreary, stultifying, and who
do not appear themselves to be unhappy, alienated, discon-
tented, dying to get away from it all, these people go to much
the same movies, and enjoy them in much the same ways, as
those who might be thought to be trying to escape dreariness.
If these people are not escaping they must be getting something else from movie-going. This suggests, what I believe
to be the case, that movies have mutliple functions.

Let us turn now to some ideas about what movies
might function as. A first and obvious one already alluded
to is vicarious experience. Lynd (1925) quotes a mother in
Middletown as saying "I send my daughter [to the movies] because a girl has to learn the ways of the world somehow and
the movies are a good safe way." The assumption here is
that we can learn from the movies informally. These are
not instructional or documentary films the daughter is going
to see. They are ordinary entertainment films in the course
of which are modeled many life situations that the ordinary
person will sooner or later face. How they are handled may
or may not in itself be exemplary, but the very act of being
able to anticipate them is valuable.

Let us now separate several ways in which this learning function of movies can be used by audiences. We are following the order in which Mendelsohn (1966) covers them, but
treating them somewhat differently. First, reference group
theory: many movie stories are not set in the groups to
which most of the audience belongs, but rather among groups
to which they would like, or even to which they aspire, to
belong. Examples are films about the rich, the powerful,

the glamorous, the successful. Such groups are reference points for the audience, who may try to act as if they were members or going to be members of such groups. One way audiences have of learning about how to do this is to see movies which feature the glamorous or the powerful. The phoniness of many Hollywood treatments of school and college rebellions is repudiated or laughed at by their potential audience because they have been to school and college and know what is shown is nonsense. However, if the young see a film about married life, if the poor see a film about the middle class, and if the films are remotely plausible, this will make concrete for them the characteristics of their reference group. Powdermaker (1950) notes that "audiences tend to accept as true that part of a movie story which is beyond their experience" (p. 13).

Associated with this function is another learning function; namely, status aspiration. Sometimes the movies will portray a way of life in such a way as to attribute to it high status. This may be one that the viewers had never really thought much about, e.g., policemen. However, insofar as there is in American life something of a permanent quest for enhanced status, this can be made especially plausible or concrete by viewing its portrayal in movies.

A further aspect of this whole matter is anticipatory socialization: those of a lower status, or those belonging to groups different from the reference groups to which they aspire, can learn from the media how those groups behave and thus begin to attempt to behave and to adopt lifestyles they have come to think are appropriate. For example, simply by observing the actors in a banquet scene handling the wine glasses and the cutlery they can learn to do similar things themselves in hopes that when one day they move up they will already be socialized. James Bond is constantly instructing (or misleading) his audiences about how to mix cocktails, which wine to drink, how to behave at a casino, with glamorous women, etc.

We now turn to a somewhat different function, inward looking rather than outward looking, namely the reinforcement of values. Gans (1962) observed Italian-Americans in Boston watching television and recorded how they screened out middle-class values and noted and approved working-class values. They liked "action" stories where the hero is loyal to his buddies and not to women. Such heroes succeed mainly because of strength, courage and cunning. Education and wealth

play no part. This is, as it were, the way the working-class
man would like to see himself--his limited capacities allowing him to enjoy adventure and success. We may wonder
whether the basic and continuing appeal of Westerns is here
explained. Skill with words, complex motives, introspection,
education, money--none of these accrue to the Western hero.
He is usually strong and silent--but he knows what is right
and is finally given the chance to act and set things straight.
A chance that rarely occurs in ordinary life.

Why do people turn to the media for this kind of reinforcement? Riesman (1950) provides a possible answer. He
suggests that formerly the primary group performed the function of teaching and reinforcing values. But now that such
traditional direction has almost disappeared, people must look
elsewhere. They look to the media, to movies, television,
mass magazines for information about how to cope with life
and to find value in it. This suggestion in itself raises serious questions, because if it is true, then there is legitimate
social concern with whether the tutelage provided by the mass
media is responsible and acceptable. Moreover, in the en-
suing twenty years other writers have raised serious questions about the alleged atrophying of the functions of the primary group, and have argued to the contrary that the school
and the media are relatively small influences on the individual. At best, then, the reinforcement sought in movies might
be explained as a comfort at a time when social change is
threatening and undermining values.

We come now to legitimation. It can be argued that
the portrayal of certain characters and ways of life in movies is suffused with approval. When this happens we call it
legitimation, making something legitimate or acceptable. When
middle-class ways are held up for all to admire this legiti-
mates the middle-class way of life. Clearly this alleged
function of movies must be in doubt. The much more detached and experimental outlook of the younger audience lends
itself to no such simple reading. My own interest was especially keen in Joe (the generation gap has grown so wide
that hard-hat and bourgeois find themselves agreeing in a
view which may destroy their children), where the hippie drug
peddler is portrayed as rather nasty--he dopes his girl friend
and ruthlessly peddles fake drugs to youngsters. Making a
pile by drugs is not legitimated by Joe. Perhaps it is in
Easy Rider (tripping on motorcycles, pot, and benevolence
across America), which opens on an ambiguous scene of a
huge trade in white powder (cocaine or heroin) which bank-

rolls the heroes' subsequent odyssey. That their entire trip is funded by a criminal if not a wicked transaction is forgotten if it was ever noticed. Curiously, there has been relatively little outcry about such incidents. Joe, however, makes the drug life unattractive. It also doesn't legitimate the final slaughter of the far-from-innocents.

Connected with legitimation is the tendency movies have to confer status on what they portray. Values and mores can be shown as unremarkable or even admirable and hence have their status enhanced. Because movies feature stars, stardom has status. Because middle-class life is extolled, it is important and worthwhile. Much of the rage evoked by the heroic portrayal of the Ku Klux Klan in Birth of a Nation (war destroys the gentle South; only the Klan is left to defend honor) was because it was felt this would confer status on an unworthy organization. One can reverse the proposition and note that movies also can withdraw status. The portrayal of blacks as menials, clowns, entertainers and very little else in white-produced American movies for 80 years may have made it more difficult for them to fight for status as equal citizens (Cripps 1967, 1977).

Many other of the functions can be reversed too. Showing the forces of law and order as corrupt or incompetent or lawless can as it were de-legitimate them, as can the portrayal of parents as confused and unsure, children as knowledgeable and certain. Values can be undermined as well as reinforced. Think of the indulgent recorded laughter received by smart-aleck children on television sit-coms. Doubtless much of the fuss surrounding movies relates to these negative aspects. Solving problems by violence in war, Western and crime films can be seen as legitimating or conferring status on violence as a solution to problems. Showing intellectuals as crooks, communists or cowards can undermine the status and authority of intellectuals. So concerned with such issues have some commentators been, that Hollywood was actually pressured by the federal government in the thirties and forties not to make villains identifiable as coming from countries towards which America was friendly (Jowett 1976, pp. 322-4).

If the legitimation/de-legitimation argument is pushed to its conclusion, an audience will have to be thought of as vacillating from film to film, its values undermined one moment, reinforced the next. But this allows us to see that of course the values to begin with must have come from other sources, and since such vacillation is not apparent, there must be other means by which the influence of movies is resisted.

Two other functions attributed to movies rely less on the content of the movies themselves than on the interaction of that content with the audience. Much movie-going is a leisure-time activity and is engaged in with companions--of choice rather than of necessity. At work one must be with other employees. At play one can be alone, or with those one chooses. Most people go to movies with someone or some group or gang. In particular, much courtship activity centers around such media as movies, television, records. Movies here perform the functions of "trying out" and of a social lubricant. The "trying out" occurs in two ways: in group interactions and in utilization of film content. At the age of courtship people are preparing to enter the roles of married person, and then parent. In going around a lot with each other (as well as love-making) the couple is beginning the processes of mutual adjustment that marriage entails. Similarly, many of the films they see will foster that process, as well as indicating to them ways in which the present roles can be played.

To claim movies are a social lubricant in a community is of course flatly to contradict those critics of the mass media who see them as solitary escape mechanisms which serve to cement together a fragmented and anomic society. Movies serve a community function: people go to movies together for a reason. Put simply: they talk about them, both in anticipation and in recollection. Movies are a bond of common experience that facilitates informal contacts between people. This makes parties, dates, friendships, neighborliness, marriage and a host of other relationships easier. Movies are something to do together and enjoy together and enjoy talking about together. Mendelsohn (1966) vividly illustrates this with regard to the teenager:

> The teen-ager typically is a marginal individual with links stretching out to two worlds--that of the child and that of the adult. Neither status is clear-cut. As a teen-ager, the individual undergoes the harrowing experience of not really belonging to any one socially recognized group in the society. Consequently, there occurs a great seeking out of commonness of experience that will serve to link him to others 'in the same boat.'

The experience of mass entertainment acts as a relatively non-threatening common focal point which in turn serves three extremely important functions for the teen-ager. First, sharing interest in the same kind of experiences makes for feelings of mutual rapport. Second, by adopting unique forms of mass entertainment (e.g., rock and roll music) teen-agers accomplish a certain temporary degree of unique status that serves to identify them--to themselves, to other teen-agers, and to the world at large. Third, by engaging in the activities of mass entertainment the teen-ager is offered mechanisms that facilitate his relationships with those teen-agers whose support he so actively seeks [p. 76].

Escape Reconsidered

Against this background it might be possible to look again at the basic assumptions behind so much popular concern with the movies: fantasy, identification and escape. We mentioned the finding that those with drab lives use the media, including the movies, in much the same way as do those with satisfactory or even glamorous and rewarding lives. Perhaps our basic mistake is in assuming that escape or fantasy is compensation for clearly identifiable complaints. An alternative view is that there is a universal need for such compensation because psychically all human life consists of sublimation, repression and frustration. Freud in his pessimistic Civilization and Its Discontents (1929) is the originator of this view in modern times, but acceptance of it is not tied to allegiance to psychoanalysis. Might it not be that there is a human need to fantasize in the same way that there is a need to sleep, or a need to dream; that coping with reality can only go on if occasionally there is a respite from it, a respite where we imagine a world with other problems, or no problems, and where the childish fantasy of omnipotence can prevail? What we do is then to act out the problems of real life in an unreal way. That they work out at all may release tension, as dreams are thought to do. More important, the world of movies, unlike dreams, is one where resolution comes no matter what we do. Thus we are able to rehearse emotional and intellectual reactions to something that happens beyond our control. What happens in movies has, however, a shape and perhaps a meaning. Our lives are very often without shape, certainly our day-to-day existence is, and we constantly worry that it is without meaning. If life is just one damn thing after another, at least that is not true of a good movie.

Before I go further a qualification is in order. Some movies did experiment with rather formless and meandering plots. Easy Rider (a rambling, cross-country tour) for much of its time, Medium Cool (a photographer confused by his various assignments), Zabriskie Point (a boy-girl encounter). To some extent these were "head" films (intended to be enjoyed while on drugs), which is another matter altogether. They were part of a very brief phase. Now, the discipline that stories have beginning, middle and end is back with us. My own reaction to the return of this discipline was a sigh of relief, for I found rambling, unstructured films boring. Why did these films enjoy their (limited) popularity? For even now they occasionally surface. They were very popular with high-school students and university undergraduates, who were at the time busily engaged in criticizing the "values" of American society, and reacting against what they saw as the restraints and repressions of their heavily structured institutions. To this it could be replied that generations of high-school students and undergraduates have gone to movies and shown no particular preference for rambling, unstructured movies, indeed, if anything, actively the reverse. Perhaps an answer to this in turn would point out that people act less on the way things are in society than on the way they see things to be. The late sixties was a time when schools and universities came to be seen widely as rigid, overstructured and hence rather repressive. At the same time as rambling movies came to the fore, rambling itself, taking off, taking trips (across country as well as on drugs) entered, one might almost say, the teenage lifestyle. Against all this there are those who will argue that society doesn't just come to be seen in new ways, that even the influence of someone or some group with a compelling new view of the world has to be explained, that what makes this new view plausible or compelling has to do with objective conditions in the society. To answer this would make the digression go on far too long.

One final function, of pleasure, or gratification, at least deserves mention before this chapter closes. This function, I am sure, has not changed at all, despite the changes in movies, and despite the restructuring of the audience. Unfortunately, very little can be said about it. It simply is a fact that movies sometimes give us immense pleasure: it is a very satisfying experience to see certain movies. Which movies are going to satisfy which people is something we have been looking at in this book. Why and how this happens remains something of a mystery. Exactly what processes within the mind a pleasing movie sets off, and how they become the experience of pleasure and satisfaction, remain matters about which psychology has little or nothing to say. It is worth noting, however, that the pleasure is discernibly different from that gained from a good play, a good book, a good television program. Those who thought the movies would oust the live theater failed to realize the two are not interchangeable. They are partial substitutes as occasions; they are hardly substitutes at all as gratifications. When one is in a mood to enjoy a play, a movie won't do. Similarly, when one wants to see a movie, viewing it on television is not an equivalent satisfaction. Pauline Kael in her brilliant essay on this (1968), analyses the differences between the two media for the viewer, and the totally different experience of movies that televison provides. To see movies soon after they were made, in the order they were made, properly spaced out, when their stars were still big, in a huge darkened movie house with an audience tuned in to the movie world of the time, cannot be replicated. Television is too casual, shows movies in jumbled up order, close together, curiously distant because made long ago and starring remote actors and actresses who mean little to us any more. So far as one can see, this will always be so. Nothing looks so dated as yesterday's "topical" movies; and nothing can so quickly make the transition to camp and be enjoyed again in new ways. A movie which is very explicit about sex (Last Tango in Paris 1972) or violence (Taxi Driver 1976) or swearing (Slap Shot 1977) is a sensation and a breakthrough at the time. Later, when successors have gone further it almost becomes a different thing. We cannot say why this happens, but we can see that it has an integrative aspect: one of the things that just happens to a regular moviegoer, and which is a cardinal aspect of his pleasure, is that he learns to maintain, sustain, alter, and play with emotional attitudes and intellectual and social interests--in movies, their stars, the society of movie fans, and society at large.

Movies are a popular art, by and large, although there are a few serious artists working in them. And popular art trades mainly in ephemera--none so much as television where much of the programming disappears the moment it is transmitted. But movies are recorded in a fixed form and so survive to be re-seen, re-evaluated and, sometimes, re-enjoyed. We can thus gain a perspective on them and ask just how reliable they are as documents about our society and its history.

NOTES

1. Documented in Herbert J. Gans, The Urban Villagers, Glencoe, N.Y.: The Free Press, 1962, especially pp. 187-96.

2. Robert Macmillan criticizes this expression, pointing to the worldwide acceptance of American popular culture (movies, jazz, hamburgers, cars, musical comedy, Coca-Cola, etc.) during the heyday of Hollywood, the cosmopolitan population of the movie colony itself, and the tendency of American movies to deal with universal human and twentieth-century themes, rather than parochial American ones. None of this, I contend, shows lack of parochialism in American culture, but I take the point about Hollywood's universalism and would, like Gans, use it as a principal explanation of the "exportability" of the Hollywood product.

3. Sergei Eisenstein, perhaps the most famous of Russian directors, had some misadventures in Hollywood in 1930 (see Montagu 1968, Seton 1952, and Soderbergh 1970).

4. Ironically, when a novelist, playwright or actor once thought to be a "serious artist" began to do things for money, the phrase "gone Hollywood" was used.

5. So he left Hollywood and worked sporadically in Europe. See Higham 1970.

6. Until the sixties most countries in the world were short of US dollars and allowed only limited amounts earned by American companies to be remitted back.

IV

MOVIES AND REALITY

The Received View

A standard assumption behind much academic and critical writing about film in the twenties, thirties and forties of this century was that commercial movies were unrealistic. They had artificial stories, unreal characters, were set in untypically lavish surroundings, and did not accurately reflect the real life situations of most people living in the societies they portrayed. Among social scientists and historians the received view of these popular movies is that they have very little value as social or historical documents. Their only value, it is felt, is to an historian of the movies. Behind this view is the idea that unrealistic movies can no more be taken seriously as documents of their times than can unrealistic women's magazine stories.

"Reality" undoubtedly is being taken in a rather naive sense in this argument. Popular films are, it is true, popular. They also do not take themselves seriously. They avoid being didactic, or trying to "say something." To some extent they trade in conventions, which are of course artificial. But none of this says that they cannot give us true and interesting information about society. Certainly it is a fact that until the mid-teens of the century most movies were set among the working classes, and since then that setting has been rare. But how accurately was working-class life portrayed? In this chapter I do not want to claim that movies were, on the whole, true-to-life. What I shall try to do is show that the received view uncritically invokes a concept of reality which is neither simple nor straightforward, and that, when we disentangle it, the movies can no longer be dismissed as a social and historical document.

To begin with, we might argue this point by defending the much-maligned women's magazine stories. A quite fascinating study, in of all places Playboy, by William Iverson

(1964) showed clearly how the contents of women's magazines in general and their fiction in particular are highly revealing of editorial attitudes and, indirectly, of readership attitudes. Movies too, as we have seen, because they are made by groups, can, in themselves and in the public reaction to them, give us much information. Little attempt has been made to get at this information. Such attempts as have been made are mostly by psychologists or those similarly inclined (Wolfenstein and Leites, Kracauer, Deming). Only since the nineteen-sixties have there been attempts by sociologists (Huaco 1965, Wright 1975) and historians (Bergman 1971, Richards 1973, Smith 1976) to use films as sources of information for general as well as social and cultural history.

Acceptance of the received view entailed that only newsreels and documentaries would be worth preserving in archives. Nowadays this argument has almost been reversed. It is the unselfconscious sociology and history contained in popular movies that makes them so valuable a primary source. Moreover, the movies themselves are an important piece of American history (Sklar 1975). Given this present mood, it is something of a problem to explain why the received view held sway for so long, and what its basis was. Its basis is found in the answers to two other questions which arise: why was lack of realism regarded as deplorable; and, is the charge of lack of realism fair?

To begin with, why did the received view that commercial movies are artificial and unrealistic hold sway for so long? Obviously, the principal reason is that it is partially true. This being so, we can see that there will be a natural confluence of the moral forces that deplore artificiality because it is not uplifting and of the aesthetic forces that deplore artificiality because it is not creatively serious. This confluence dominated serious writing about movies until well into the nineteen-fifties. It is not easy to explain why the hegemony was broken. Moralistic interest switched to television at the very time that strong attacks on the received view were coming from French critics. They forced upon the world a reappraisal of the American commercial movie. Once those movies were no longer dismissed en bloc and unexamined, but, rather, examined closely, it quickly became apparent that the received view was only superficially true. A film like The Private Lives of Elizabeth and Essex (1939) may be an historical travesty, and contain anachronisms like American accents and idioms; it nevertheless is a film made in 1939, in Hollywood, by a highly professional group tuned in to the times. It tells us many things about America then--presuppositions buried so deep they were not noticeable at the time.

Now to the basis of the received view: what is wrong with artificiality, and is the charge fair?

A lack of reality in movies was considered unfortunate for at least two main reasons, one to do with the audience, the other to do with the nature of the film medium itself. The reasoning about the audience will be familiar enough to readers of Chapter I. Commercial entertainment films encourage people to escape from the problems of their lives, to live in dreamland. Audiences are thus not helped to face and cope with life's problems; indeed, they may have their energies and interest distracted from those problems, resulting in their sinking into a sort of lassitude. Now, films, as the art of the masses, surely have the responsibility to inform the masses, not to distract them; to help them cope with problems, not run away from them. No time need be spent on this argument now. In Chapter III we saw that the argument about escapism is a somewhat partial, not to say superficial, reading of the myriad functions movies can and do serve in people's lives.

The other main reason for criticizing the lack of realism in the commercial cinema is an aesthetic argument turning on the nature of photography. A camera, it is said, is a recording instrument. So photography is an art which utilizes a recording instrument. What the camera can do that drawing, painting and other visual arts cannot do, is capture exactly what is set before it in the three-dimensional world in two-dimentional pictures that appear three-dimensional. Cinematography adds to photography the capacity to capture movement. Film is thus perfectly suited to capturing the texture of life. It can achieve, in Kracauer's phrase, the redemption of physical reality. If then, film is not to copy the other visual arts, it should concentrate on what its special qualities allow it and it alone to do, that is, accurately portray the real world.

Now, is the charge fair?

Critique of the Received View

The received view is that commercial fiction films are artificial and empty. In criticism I shall suggest that there

is no requirement on the movies to be real, and no special
connection between cinematography and reality. To begin
with, what about the filmmaker? Are filmmakers like Orson
Welles, Walt Disney, John Ford, Alfred Hitchcock setting
out to portray the real world? Should they be? One might
counter suggest that they are creating a world of their imagination rather than portraying any world they or we live in
or could have lived in. Artists are also sometimes said to
be doing such things as capturing the truth of fleeting moments of experience, or recapturing emotion in tranquility.
But reality? Even the surface reality of things might better
be captured in trompe l'oeil painting, or hi-fidelity recording,
than on film. As to deeper reality: what is it, and how is
it to be captured by the camera?

Different questions can be raised about the special
claims that are being made about the nature of photography.
Certainly the lens, the sensitive emulsion, and the chemical
processes involved, all work mechanically. But so do the
pencil and brush held in the artist's hands. What the artist
does with his pencil, how he moves his brush are what counts.
How the photographer points his camera, which lens he uses,
at what setting, and how the film is processed are what count
in film. Amateur films of real events, such as parties and
holidays, are mostly much duller than the events themselves
were. This is because they are artless: the mechanics of
the medium are not controlled by the artistic purpose of attempting to realize a work of the imagination.

Hence, one might be tempted to conclude that as far
as reality goes films are documents, like paintings or pieces
of writing, which were created with imagination and must be
interpreted with imagination. There is no direct contact of
film with reality; no special communication of reality through
film. An absorbing documentary film often involves as much
.art (and artifice) as a fictional feature film: in some ways
more. The Sorrow and the Pity (1972), Marcel Ophuls' four-
hour film about Nazi collaboration in one French town, took
years to make, involving countless artistic decisions. The
world of our imagination is partial and incomplete and hence
can be realized. But the so-called real world is infinitely
large and varied, and so the problem of reproduction becomes:
which parts of it to select as sufficient to convey it all. Obviously, none is; therefore, it can never be fully conveyed.
All pictures of reality are partial, incomplete interpretations.
So, the idea that film is a unique historical document that
records events as they actually happened has to be qualified

by the realization that film is a document, like any other, which captures only an aspect of an event, not the whole truth. Experts at utilizing written documents to write history will not be able to turn to film without learning how to use it too: to "read" it critically (Smith 1976, Jarvie 1978).

A more fruitful way to look at the relations between movies and reality might be this. Movies create their own reality. A movie maker is constituting a world fused from elements in the so-called real world (as he or she sees it), and the selection and photographing of such parts of it as he chooses. Thus a movie shows a world of the creator's imagining. To explore this view it will be necessary for us to look again and in more detail at the relationship between a film and what it films, and at the notion of reality itself, for there are many-layered confusions everywhere.

Whenever a scene is captured by a camera two human acts intervene. The first is <u>selection</u>. From the flux of experience the creator selects a moment or a series of them; from the visual and aural phenomena he selects those to be recorded by the microphone, those to be framed by the camera. Once on film and tape he can make further selection; he can edit; he can process in different ways and he can combine ("mix") sound and picture as he sees fit. Selection is abetted by another act: <u>interpretation</u>. We are so used to looking at photographs and "reading" what's there, that we forget that the relationship between a scene and a photograph of it is a series of conventions built into the mechanics of the camera, which we must have mastered and compensated for before the photograph can be "read" as a representation of a recognizable three-dimensional object like a human face or a garden. All this is as true of motion pictures as it is of still photographs. Problems of perspective and framing are added to problems of editing and other kinds of emphasis. As we argued in the first chapter, movies are "read" by an active and interpreting mind, not just passively viewed or absorbed (Wilson 1961).

Let us contrast the passive and the active models of movie viewing. The passive model has a man gazing at the screen. On the screen appear certain images and from behind it come certain sounds. These impose themselves on his sense organs and thence on his brain. Figure 1 illustrates.

The active model, which we espouse in this book, looks at matters differently. A mind confronts a screen.

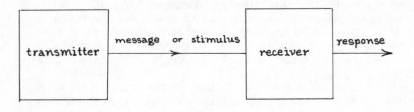

Figure 1

THE DIRECT INFLUENCE THEORY

Visual and aural information comes to it, is selected, interpreted or organized into meaningful sounds and images: the
meaning is not, as it were, there for all to see. Given common
culture and language most viewers will reconstruct the intended meaning, but that they are engaged in this <u>activity</u> must
not be forgotten. See Figure 2.

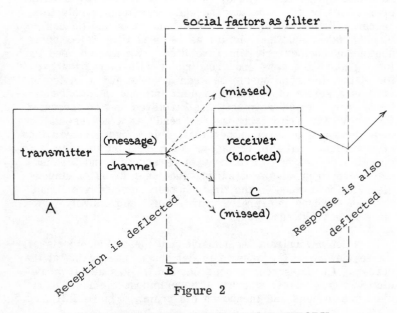

Figure 2

THE SELECTIVE PERCEPTION THEORY

The message from A is deflected at the dotted line B. This results in the deflection of some messages to such an extent that they miss their target; the viewer does not get the point. Some that reach the target are blocked by personal idiosyncracy C. What gets through is also deflected at C by the personal equation, as is the response (a person trying to be nice comes across aggressive, for example), which is further bent by social factors at B. This model is still very rudimentary.

What the viewer "sees" is the highly selected and interpreted result of the effect of a set of stimuli on his senses. In his immediate surroundings there is the fact that he is sitting in the dark in a large building surrounded by other people. His seeing of the screen cannot be divorced from that context. (But of course there is in addition a much wider context.) This is not just a solitary observer. This man is himself a product of a society, along with certain of its institutions and is affected by them, stands in certain of its traditions, and understands its conventions. All of this mass of background is present in his viewing. It is, so to say, articulated in the process of that viewing. These remarks should dispel the naive notions of film viewing which lie behind the clamor for realism in the cinema. Realism is an interesting artistic aim, but one which is no more suited to film than it is to any other art medium.

The next question we need to look into is the reality behind the realism. When we demand of film that it be realistic, there is a hidden transitive: realistic relative to what: other films, other media, to reality itself? Which aspect of reality itself? The reality of things, i.e., the physical surface; the reality of emotion, i.e., the feeling tones of things? And, anyway, how are we to judge whether one or another attempt at any of these things is the more realistic? In countries where "socialist realism" is demanded, the problem is solved. Art which advances socialism is more realistic than art which does not. How do we know which art advances socialism? Simple: the vanguard of socialism will tell us. What is the vanguard of socialism? Why, the Party, of course. For those of us not of the Faith, the problem is less easy to resolve and criteria are harder to come by.

Do we mean by reality anything that "really" is in front of a camera? This is doubtful. The plasterboard simulation of a street or house stands in front of the camera in a Hollywood studio. In a certain sense it is a real thing:

part of the reality of the physical world. In another sense
it is completely unreal or fake. It is not a street or a house,
it only appears to be. Reality is usually contrasted with
mere appearance. So the way things look is not reality, and
when we concern ourselves with realism in the cinema, we
must not be misled by the physical surface of things. This
applies also to newsreels and documentaries. Newsreel shots
of a war, or of a politician, or of real city streets are not
necessarily going to yield a realistic movie. They may be
edited together with jazzy music, or overlaid with a tendentious commentary. The end results may be in one case a
satire, in another, propaganda. Even without such selection
and interpretation, however, the raw footage does not capture
the real. The real is not given; what is the real is something
we have to judge. War material showing men being killed
may be horrifying; it equally well may be distant and leave
us cold. There are those who would declare both films unrealistic. Killing, they might say, is really horrifying only
in an unjust war. Others might declare that just or unjust
all war is horrifying and a presentation with a very distant
perspective is inherently unreal. The concept of reality gets
too slippery to handle.

So reality can mean or be: what the Party says, part
of the physical world, what is hidden behind appearances,
genuine as opposed to fake, truth as opposed to lies, spon-
taneous as opposed to staged, and so on. As the can of
worms is opened up, one must come seriously to doubt the
value of claiming for film or even for photography generally
any special connection with reality, any special proclivity
for realism.

Clearly, whether or not we construe a piece of film
as realistic will turn on our belief as to what the truth about
things is. If we feel the film depicts the truth, we will say
it is realistic. Even if the film presents truthfully the way
we see things, then presents truthfully the way others see
things, and says that it is difficult to decide between competing views, we will not withhold the honorific of realism
from it. But then it should be remembered that we will often declare a poem, a novel or a painting realistic, and here
we may be contrasting it with fantasy. For realism may be
an artistic style, so that even a work we find to be utterly
false in its particulars, we may be forced to call realistic,
because that is the stylistic mode the artist is operating in.
This is the case with postwar Italian movies, which called
themselves "neo-realistic." They wanted to make films about

the poor, oppressed, and forgotten members of Italy's society. They used the streets of the city, everyday stories, and non-professional actors. But the script, the camera, the music, the editing were all contrivances carefully used to put over a particular view of these matters held by the creators.

That the neo-realists used amateur actors, that others sometimes use actors and have them improvise, might also be called into question as a device aimed at realism. Realism is not just reproduction of the surface of things, as we have seen. Hence, the attempt to reproduce the way people speak, to get rid of the consciously "technical" actor can be seen to be naive. Reality is not out there beyond the "barriers" of camera, actors, contrived scripts and lines, sets, etc. Reality is something the filmmaker creates. Even if the filmmaker is trying to recreate actual events, all he is in fact doing is staging or restaging the events as he understands them, recreating what he thinks happened (however much evidence he collects, ultimately he has to select what he thinks is the true story). Instructive in this way is the film Z. Concerned with the assassination of a leftish Greek politician sometime before the right-wing colonels' coup, it contrives to be both a thriller and a film to rev the audience up against the politics and violence of those who plot the assassination. It draws heavily on what it is generally agreed happened, but it also subtly changes, compresses, and simplifies in order to drive its point home. Its makers doubtless believe that in essence it is a truthful film, even if some of the detail is invented or distorted. More sceptical viewers have said that the urge to make a thriller, with "goodies" and "baddies" on clearly defined opposite sides, and to stage exciting pieces of action as well as an investigation of what happened, somehow have become uppermost in the director's mind and hence the film will not for example be taken as a serious document by future historians of Greek politics of the period.

Perhaps this discussion is too elaborate for my purposes. Perhaps all that those who claim the film has a special affinity for reality mean is that film can show us the world beyond the walls of the film studio, the world of everyday living. We will not understand this claim, or that of the neo-realists, or that of the documentary movement, if we do not set it in the context of the typical feature movie of the time. British and Italian movies of the thirties, for example, were rightly ridiculed as "white telephone" movies, because they seemed to take place in a dreamy limbo of artificial people with artificial concerns, and elegant and luxurious surroundings. Westerns, musicals, romances poured from Hollywood as escape entertainment, and they were thought to bear no more relation to the world of everyday living than did the pap that was served up as fiction in women's magazines. This was the view of things which, as we have seen, people take who tried to argue for the use of the film to capture the texture of real life, to concern itself with reality, not with escape. So we come back to the initial contrast: reality versus escape. Crusaders are always blind to the diversity of things. Some musicals, Westerns, romances, were superb films. Moreover, documentaries, neo-realistic films, serious social dramas could sometimes be very earnest and humorless, however true and real. And there is unrealism here too. Life even at its hardest for people in Western society is rarely without humor or romance. Hence the relevance of these elements in films. Supose that life is boring. This is not to be conveyed by making a film of life that is itself a bore to the audience. Somehow, the tedium must be conveyed by artistic means, that is, by exploiting the conventions and resources (which is to say the artificialities) of the film medium. People do not live their lives in the cinema. If the filmmaker wants his audience to stay in their seats he must keep them interested, otherwise they will fall asleep or turn their attention elsewhere. They are at the movies to enjoy themselves. They expect a story. If the texture of their lives is reproduced without any dramatic or other points of interest, even if they agree with the propaganda, then they will likely, as we say nowadays, "turn off."

I admitted, in Chapter III, that we did not know what entertained people. But we do know they enjoy some things and not others, and this is relevant. We can't simply look at any film, however obscure, and declare that as a group product it tells us something of the social reality from which it stems. Some critical attention will need to be paid to how it was received, what kind of rapport it established with its audience. But we must add neither the extreme view that the audience has rapport only with what it perceives as true, nor the extreme view that the audience enjoys only the fantasy into which it can escape.

All the issues surrounding film and reality eventually come back to this basic axis between reality and truth. Where is the room for art? Where is the room for imagination? Ever more imaginative presentation of a line of

propaganda is not a situation we want to promote. If the film
is an art that uses photography as its raw material, so is
the novel an art which uses words as its raw material. Certainly the imagination of the spectator is used in quite different ways by the film and the novel. The novel can be very
exact about what was said, about what has happened elsewhere
in time and space, about what was thought, about the overall scheme of things, because the page can always be turned
back. Film lays down the sight and sound of things exactly,
but tells us little of interior lives and gives us little sense
of the scheme of things. Each medium has a number of resources available to creators to realize a world of their imagination, of their mind (even if they claim that the world they
are conjuring is as close a replica as they can manage of
some event that actually happened). Such truth and reality
as they achieve must be connected in certain ways with the
vigor and coherence of these imaginative constructions. The
further reference, from the imaginative constructions outwards
to the world (compare the move from a coherent linguistic
system to the question of whether anything said in it corresponds to what is the case), is problematic. For while it is
true to say of artistic creations that they seek truth, it is
not at all clear that they seek documentary truth. And when we
consider cartoons and musicals it is difficult to know just
what sort of truth is being sought. Truths about human nature? Perhaps. Not, at any rate, propositional truths, because of the artist's standard reply to the question, "What
does your work mean, what does it say?": namely, "If there
was any other way of saying it than by creating the work, I
should have done that."

Perhaps enough has been said now to show that the
thesis about a special connection between movies and reality
is very cloudy, since realism can have any number of contrasts, and also very peculiar, because movies from their
earliest times have been all the things we have distinguished.
They have been naturalistic (newsreels and early "actualities"
as they were called); realistic (attempting to capture the truth
rather than the surface of things); false (in that they have mis-
represented the world); lies (intentional misrepresentation, particularly propaganda); and fantasy (Méliès, science fiction,
cartoons, musicals). Why any of these categories, all of
which have been of interest to the movie-going public, should
be singled out as the true nature or correct mode in which
movies should be made is puzzling. The explanation I offer
has to do with morality and politics.

Why Realism?

Has mass art any special responsibility to represent the viewpoint and the social and political interest of the masses? Many writers on film seem to have thought so.

The call for realism in art is one peculiar to the intellectuals of this century, a century in which socialism and egalitarianism have been rife. Intellectuals who have turned their attention to the mass media have been of two kinds: those who have come to them with contempt, regarding them as the opium of the masses; and those who have looked upon them with joy, as an entree to the minds of the masses. Those particularly interested in getting inside the minds of the masses were perhaps political radicals. Lenin is notorious for having said that a crucial artistic medium for Bolsheviks was the movies--that through the movies the reconstruction of society, presentation of the history of the revolution, and improvement of class-consciousness would be achieved. In the twenties in the Soviet Union this doctrine worked in practice in a very exciting way. Eisenstein, Pudovkin and Dovzhenko were allowed enormous freedom to experiment with styles and techniques--even if one might cavil that the content of their films was almost unrelievedly political and revolutionary. But, this was immediately after the most important upheaval in Europe since the French Revolution, and a preoccupation with its background, its causes, and its events is perhaps understandable. Socialist realism was also allowed to help in the collectivization movement (when the Russian government tried to force reluctant peasants to band together in collectives). But the snag was that as long as movies that presented entertainment, fantasy, and humor were allowed to be imported from abroad, the public by and large preferred them to the didactic and instructional films made by the Party intellectuals. As a result, the régime had slowly to exclude these foreign films. But then a further problem presented itself: were the domestic movies too propagandist or didactic, people would stop going to see them. Hence, such movies would not even recoup their production costs. And at this point, in an impoverished economy, serious and hard decisions were to be faced and the result was the reintroduction of let us say, ordinary entertainment movies none too closely governed by the principles of socialist realism (Leyda 1960, Rimberg 1959).

Socialist realism can best be characterized as art which aims to be realistic, or art which presents reality as a socialist sees it, or, perhaps even better, art which presents reality as a socialist wants to see it or wants it to be. ("Socialist" here being, of course, code for "communist.") These last two qualifications expose the nonsense of the whole notion. Anyone who has seen the heroic statues of muscled workers and peasants in the squares of Russia, China and the satellite countries, and the similar styles of painting, will know that this formula has been debased.

Perhaps this was realized fairly early on by intellectuals, and as a result in the thirties in Britain there grew up the so-called documentary movement which was begun largely by intellectuals and which acknowledged great debts to the Soviet cinema, and which took as its basic premise not socialist realism but the "creative interpretation of actuality." Some of the films were propaganda (like Housing Problems 1935), but some of them were evocations of a place (like Song of Ceylon 1934), or an ordinary event (like the Night Mail train going from London to Glasgow, 1936). This tradition of movie making has I think been more influential on the mainstream of commercial cinema than have the oddities of socialist realism.

Since movie-going is in all countries a voluntary activity and can hardly be envisaged as anything else, all movie makers have to face the fundamental problem that their audience must want to go to see their movies and, once the show has begun, want to sit through to the end. Thus, whatever the filmmakers' aims--realism, naturalism, propaganda, socialist realism, fantasy--they must start from entertainment. Entertainment need not be regarded as a frivolous matter. One might say that Shakespeare or Beethoven is entertaining. Plato is entertaining to a philosopher or even to anyone interested in the questions he is discussing. A book of science or mathematics at its best should be entertaining. Entertainment can mean no more than engaging and pleasurable to the mind or the heart. This does not preclude some difficulty, some things that may be at first unpalatable. The creator must bear in mind that in a mass art without a tradition he cannot rely on the audience to come to him, he must go out and seize its attention. The evidence all bears this out. There are naturalistic films that are immensely entertaining, like the early actualities of coronations and so on and of course like newsreels, which, although they are edited, are sometimes very little edited. There are entertaining "realistic" pictures, like the British documentaries and like many semidocumentary films, like some of the neo-realistic films of Italy, like the kitchen-sink realism school of Britain in the sixties. There have been entertaining propaganda films, like the so-called documentaries that Leni Riefenstahl made for the Nazis and some of the war documentaries made for propaganda purposes in America like the "Why We Fight" series. And there have, of course, been many entertaining fantasies from the cartoons of Felix the Cat right through to the full-scale satirical musical of MGM in its heyday. Good filmmakers have not needed to be taught that they must entertain. They have always proceeded first to seek an audience and provide it with something attractive before imposing their theories of what a film should be.

Many of the ideas about movies and reality I have been discussing were held by people who were anti-American. Among them were Americans, naturally. All were actively hostile to the mainstream of the American cinema, which they saw as capitalistic, monopolistic, powerful, successful and above all dominated by a desire to please and hold on to the public. Yet, curiously enough, there have been two traditions in American movies which do not fit well with the image of mercenary escapist content. These two traditions are, first, of movies that crusade against crime and corruption and, second, of movies which praise America and strike patriotic and anticommunist attitudes. These days it is easy to show great interest in the first and to be contemptuous of the second. This may be because some examples of the second, like Big Jim McLain (FBI man John Wayne and sidekick James Arness, who hate Commies, clean up a cell of them on Hawaii, 1952), or The Green Berets (John Wayne fights for the freedom of South Vietnam, 1968--is it a coincidence that they both star John Wayne?) have been unfortunate. It is easy to forget a film like James Thurber's The Male Animal. Made in 1942 and starring Henry Fonda and Jack Carson, this is the story of a timid college professor who is visited simultaneously by his wife's former lover, a great football hero, and by an academic crisis of conscience. He insists upon freedom of thought in his classroom and especially on his right to read out radical documents (Sacco and Vanzetti) in the course of discussing them. The issue is resolved by his not being fired, but by general acclaim and the regaining of his wife's respect--though not at the time of the reading of the documents.

Twenty-odd years later, Shirley MacLaine and Peter Ustinov starred in John Goldfarb Please Come Home (1964), a vicious satire on among other things CIA overflights (shades of the Powers affair[1]), State Department incompetence, toadying to Middle Eastern potentates from whom America wants something, and the cynical use of innocent bystanders. (U-2 pilot "wrong way Goldfarb" fixes up a deal with a despot by training a football team to "beat" Notre Dame.) Just a résumé of its plot makes one wonder how on earth it was made. But made it was (by 20th Century-Fox), and as part of the American popular cinema.

By the tradition of patriotic and praise-America films I mean films in which not only are reactionary ideas expressed but in which ideas are expressed that go back to the ideas of the founding fathers and the revolution which created the United States: the ideas of freedom, equality before the law, freedom of the press, freedom of religion and political belief, etc. Perhaps because the country was founded by idealistic men with a high view of the perfectability of human nature, the society also has this strong journalist tradition of ruthless self examination--principally in the daily press.

The press in America has had a tremendous role in the exposure of crime and corruption at all levels of government and society. (The Watergate exposures of grave malpractice in government, including the FBI and the CIA, all owe a great deal to the press--even if All the President's Men, 1976, overrates The Washington Post and underrates Judge Sirica.) This tradition has passed over into movies. It would be tedious to recite a long list. Three well-known examples will have to suffice. The Grapes of Wrath (1940) is a film about rural poverty in the Oklahoma dust bowl. The soil blows away, the banks repossess, and, through great hardship, the family migrates to California. Little Caesar (1931) chronicles the rise of Johnny Rico from small-time hoodlum and enforcer until he is at the top of the underworld. But others are greedy too and he is shot by rivals. The Manchurian Candidate (1962) is a mysterious tale of how an American POW in Korea is brainwashed and programmed to assassinate, years later, a US politician at a crucial moment when a secret communist dupe will be able to take over.[2] Story formulas such as that of the small-town journalist who discovers and tries to expose corruption, or of the young boy who is corrupted by various evil forces bearing down upon him--these are staples of the American protest film. Most of the gangster films of the nineteen thirties and the films about prisons and the need for reform of them (e.g., I Am a Fugitive from a Chain Gang--once wrongly convicted, a man can never clear his name, 1932) and films against the

FAWZIA فوزي

1 ١

Sixties films contained plenty of social criticism. A neglected example being the 20th Century-Fox production of John
Goldfarb, Please Come Home (1964). Shirley MacLaine is
in the harem of Peter Ustinov as a reporter. Soon a U-2
pilot, "Wrong-Way Goldfarb," will crash nearby and compli-
cate the State Department's maneuvering to get an air base.
A British director, J. Lee Thompson, worked from the script
by William Peter Blatty, who would later achieve somewhat
greater success when he wrote The Exorcist. Compared to
this U-2 fiasco satire, Watergate has yet to provoke a movie
anything remotely as savage, although Nasty Habits (1977)
aspires to be.

---

death sentence and lynching like Fury (mob lynches the wrong
man, 1936), and You Only Live Once (innocent man sent to
jail becomes a killer, 1937)--all these films, which were
made in greater quantity by Warner Brothers than any other
studio--pitilessly examined gross faults in American society
and its deviation from its own ideals.

Whether a film like I Am a Fugitive from a Chain Gang could ever be made in any other foreign country is much to be doubted. France has yet to film Zola's J'Accuse (Hollywood has treated it twice, in The Life of Emile Zola, 1937, and I Accuse, 1958; Papillon, 1973, is the latest in a long line of American films exposing French prison conditions), Britain has yet to make a film about its corrupt policemen or bullying civil servants, the Philby spy scandal, or other embarrassments. The poverty and limited horizons of much of British society have not been exposed in films. A sensational scandal like the Profumo affair would never be the subject of a film. Hence, to the outside world, and perhaps to the surprise of Americans, the film industry in the United States seems to represent a vigorously self-critical tradition; and hence also the vitality and critical outlook of the films of the late sixties is not so much a surprise as an interesting revival and strengthening of a tradition. It remains to be seen what happens next.

In sum, then, my explanation of the realism dispute is this. Whether intellectuals were contemptuous of the media or hoped to use them for propaganda, they had no use for the popular cinema, which meant, by and large, the American cinema. Most films came from America, most popular style was set in the States. This merely compounded the anti-Americanism so long rife among intellectuals (and especially left-wing intellectuals) in Europe. One camp saw realism as a means of raising the movies to the level of education, and even of art. The other camp saw realism as a means of exposing the rottenness of the system, its crises, wars, etc., and hence of raising the class-consciousness of the masses. In effect these two camps become one, and sometimes their arguments are fused in a single individual. However, the blatant manipulation of the philosophy of realism into the artificialities and lies of socialist realism in communist countries, and the evidently critical tradition in American movies, has made little impact upon theorists of realism. Their pet ideas will perhaps be buried with them, for it is noticeable that the new generation of writers about film do not accept the gospel of realism at all.

In my university film classes these days, I am constantly being told by students that they like today's films because they are more true, or more realistic, more honest than those of the past. To some extent the students' attitude can be explained away as the result of sheer ignorance of the films of the past. For a generation passionately interested in film, and full of potential Virginia Mayo specialists, there are yawning gaps in their knowledge. Another explanation might be the usual tendency to confuse the newest with the best. Yet, withal, there may be something in what they say. College students are mainly interested in sex and politics, and in these two areas, recent films have been bolder and more explorative than in the past, as the censors have withered, and as film audiences have become more sophisticated and receptive. We have already reviewed some of the trends in films about relations between the sexes. More could be said. Goodbye, Columbus (woo the Jewish princess and you get entangled in her web of guilts, 1969) and Summer of '42 (shy adolescent gets sexual initiation from recent war widow, 1972), brought birth control devices into the story; Carnal Knowledge (two American men have very different but equally unsatisfactory sexual careers) brought the condom onto the screen in the course of exploring the whole question of the female in American male sex fantasies.[3] But along with this urge for reality we find a new nostalgia--Patton (the career of a brilliant but unbalanced American tank commander in World War II, 1970), Summer of '42, and The Wild Bunch (a gang of outlaws in the Wild West is gradually whittled away by the advance of technology, 1969) reveal strong yearnings for a lost past. Present-day movies about the lost past: Catch 22 (horrors of World War II send a soldier out of his mind, so he sets out for Sweden, 1970), about World War II but really about Vietnam; M.A.S.H. (comedy about a mobile advanced surgical hospital), about Korea but again really about Vietnam; sometimes get everything mixed up. Other movies are filled with clips from old movies: Morgan (working-class artist goes mad when his girl marries someone pukka, 1966), Myra Breckenridge (a man who has had a sex-change operation makes a career in Hollywood, 1970), Summer of '42, and The Last Picture Show (the lights are going out in the movie theaters of small towns all over Texas, 1971). Is this a new way of being old movie buffs? If so, the problem arises, why is the present generation so interested in old movies?

NOTES

1. Early in May 1960, just before a scheduled Paris summit meeting between Khrushchev and Eisenhower, Francis Gary Powers, the pilot of a U-2 spy plane, was shot down over the USSR. He was on a mission for the CIA. Eisenhower refused to apologize for the overflights, on the grounds

that espionage was a distasteful necessity. A furious Khrushchev abandoned the summit and cancelled Eisenhower's trip
to Russia.

    2. Executive Action (1973), is a film which suggests
that a small group of right-wing plotters were responsible
for Kennedy's assassination; The Parallax View (1974) postu-
lates a whole CIA-type organization that specializes in political assassination; while Three Days of the Condor (1975)
overtly suggests that agencies of the CIA engage in flagrantly
illegal mayhem. A fascinating sub-Theme is the fear of
military take-over as in Seven Days in May (1964) and Twi-
light's Last Gleaming (1977)

    3. Or take a vicious attack on stereotyped sex roles
like The Stepford Wives (directed by Bryan Forbes, from a
script by Ira Levin, 1974). Real suburban housewives are
gradually replaced by compliant robots. Only the heroine
and her friend notice.

V

MOVIES AS SOCIAL CRITICISM

Our argument in this book has been that the social psychological functions of movies have not changed a great deal; they were always multifarious. The early concern with the movies' influence on personality formation and socialization died a premature death with the supervention of television. Little or no evidence of serious influence has yet been turned up.[1] But the group dynamics of movies have changed and the changes are interesting. To begin with, the audience group: from originally being a working-class recreation, the movie audience by the nineteen-twenties became a cross-section of American society characterized by the middle-class outlook and expectations which dominate the society, and that audience has now changed again into the youth of the society, embodying their outlook. From novelty audience it became a habit audience and has now made the transition to being something of an occasion audience. From looking to movies to startle and amuse, the audience has increasingly come to look to movies to shock and amaze (Jaws 1976, King Kong 1976). Movies have shifted from being dominant in the consciousness of the audience, for most people the main form of commercial entertainment, to being only one of a number of alternatives.

The industry as a group has changed too. Beginning as a fly-by-night operation of frantic improvization and shaky financing (to 1909), it became a prosperous, well-tooled, mass-production monopoly (1909-1960), and then changed again into a more particularized yet once-again shaky business. Where once a studio was a group of highly skilled professionals who were shuffled into ad hoc teams for each movie, teams are now drawn together with no studio discipline of apprenticeship or working together whatever. Where once the studios were hierarchies ruled over by experienced showmen, they are now bossed by young executives as much dependent on their financier overlords as on any show-business experience. With the product no longer mass produced, the studios no longer in control of theaters, each movie has to be planned separately and its particular audience carefully

156

aimed at. Gans's idea that subcultural programming would be profitable has transpired: each movie is in a way subculturally programmed to a constituency: diverse successes like Mary Poppins (nanny with magical powers), The Sound of Music (an Austrian family becomes a singing group), Love Story (girl and boy fall in love, girl dies), Airport (airport as a setting for soap opera), The Godfather (the rituals of life, death and succession to office in the Mafia), Death Wish (muggers should be discouraged with their own tactics), The Exorcist (the Devil is alive and active in Georgetown), Jaws (summer fun is spoiled by a man-eater) show that careful calculation about what audiences want is not a lost art.

The net result of these changes in the viewing and producing groups is that the film fare available in the average large city in North America is now unprecedentedly diverse. There will, as a rule, be on offer: pornography, skin flicks, sensational or horror triple bills, revivals of old movies, Continental movies, a blockbuster musical in a long run, repertory and season houses, and a selection of new movies that ranges from undisturbing and star-studded movie equivalents of a "good read" to the most provocative and outlandish attacks on everything the society stands for. From this barrage of goodies the taste subcultures can, as it were, select out the menu that suits them and ignore the rest. Thus one hears less complaint about movies these days, although they are more violent and pornographic than was common in the forties. Censor boards in many cities are practically phasing themselves out of existence. Those who enjoy seeing movies that are reassuring and rather old-fashioned can readily do so. Those who expect movies to tackle many of the issues fudged on television can also find them. Regardless of how people want movies to function for them, they can get what they want.

Of special interest to this volume are those movies which became symbols of the protest movement of the late sixties. How ironic that the medium which struggled for forty years to avoid proper social controls, and was finally tamed in 1934, should burst out again in the late sixties and immediately be capable of producing both Easy Rider (drug dealing finances cross-country motorcycle quest for the Holy Grail) and Mary Poppins (hymn to the English nanny). How interesting that movies, while becoming a minority interest, have also remained a majority interest. When pictures like The Graduate (love cures boredom) or Love Story (love is not killed by death) or The Godfather (tradition is stronger than education) or Jaws (nature red in tooth and tooth), become hits, they take unprecedented sums of money. [2]

Is the Situation Stable?

Having generalized about the present situation, the
question now is to ask whether this situation will continue
and if not, what changes are likely to come about. In particular, is the "pendulum theory" true in this area? This
theory states that social change is not always continuous progress in one direction, but may take the form of swings back-
ward and forward between extremes. These swings in particular are often invoked as examples: the extremes of free
expression and dissent versus muffling and tight control; of
allowing displays of sex and violence as opposed to totally
banning them. Many are those who direly predict that a
permissive decade will be followed by a repressive one. But
maybe they are carried away by a metaphor, the metaphor of
the pendulum. Maybe the new freedom to express and explore
has to do with underlying changes in the social structure, not
just the swinging to and fro of public opinion, and maybe
these changes are as permanent as anything ever is in society. To begin with, let us look first at the changes internal
to the movie industry.

Movies are a business. They constantly search for
consumers to buy their product, namely an audience. As
long as creative individuals can turn out financially successful movies they are going to get the chance to do so. In an
uncertain market the businessman must take chances. There
is also no reason to believe that as executives get younger
and more sophisticated they might not themselves enjoy the
diversity and provocativeness of movies. Hence they will
have both commercial and personal reasons for continuing
the openended exploration of the movie market.

Look now at the audience and the offerings. The a-
mount of leisure time at their disposal grows, the amount of
money they allocate to recreation grows. The number of ways
they can spend their money also grows. Movies, radio, television, theater, sports, bowling, travel, and hosts of other
outlets present themselves. When they choose to go to the
show it had better be something acceptable, or next time
they'll spend their money in other ways.

A new balance is working its way out in the society.
Extreme attitudes of permissiveness and repression exist,
but the band in the middle is now much wider. Radicalism--
whether sexual or political--is no longer unthinkable, still
less reprehensible. Americans are allowed to think the

thought that America is not God's own country, is not without other than minor faults, is not the best of all possible worlds (Easy Rider, gentleness is met with violence; Medium Cool, violence pervades the society, Dirty Harry and Death Wish, violence breeds violence).   Extremists go the other way and argue that America is evil, the worst of all possible worlds, fissured by enormous faults and scarcely noticeable virtues (Zabriskie Point, only random living and sex can blow it from your mind).   Both extreme praise and extreme condemnation are just that--extreme.   But at least if both are tolerated a critical dialogue can go on.   If the subject of sex is allowed to come to the surface of consciousness, and be talked about and explored, many of its problems may straighten themselves out.   If widely differing views are tolerated then some sort of a discussion can begin about what is right and what is wrong.   The key is the decline of puritanism and the rise of liberalism in America.   America has always been officially liberal, and institutionally liberal, but its ideology has been puritan and its politics often populist.   America's founders knew what was wrong with Europe, her immigrants knew that America was a great place where everything was fine and dandy.   To the outside world America's attitudes to international politics have long been regarded as moralistic and domineering.   This is seen as a result of the winning out of puritanism and populism over liberalism.   The alternative tradition of liberalism and pragmatism has often been worsted.   Now, at last, it seems to be gaining the upper hand.   Much of this must have to do with the harsh experiences of world wars and international politics.   Much also with the decline of organized religious beliefs and the self-righteousness which so often goes with it.   Still more must it have to do with the revolution of rising expectations.   The abject poor do not ask why they are poor.   The poor who are getting less so begin to ask, "If we can be this much better off, why not still more so?"   Organized labor fought its battles and certainly improved its lot.   But somehow puritan ideology prevented strong pressure for a welfare state's succeeding.   The impetus that finally forced the realization that America was deeply flawed was the way in the affluent fifties the racism problem focussed the conflict between a liberal and egalitarian ideology on the one hand, and discrimination against blacks and others both in institutions and in practical attitudes on the other hand.   We will look at that in the last section.

For the moment, then, America's movies are critically self aware.   It is an uncomfortable state, but one never

ceases to be surprised by America's capacity to experiment.
Part of this critical self-awareness is the notion that diversity (racial, religious, cultural, regional, ethnic, sexual,
generational) is deep and proper. Part of it also is that
America needs to minister to herself as well as others. Ar-
ticulation of this critical self-awareness can thus spread from
the intellectual coteries where it has always existed, to the
mass media, where waits the mass audience, excited, dis-
turbed, expectant. In particular there waits that semi-myth-
ical figure, Youth. For the most part "Youth" is rather lost
and bewildered: neither school nor parents seeming to have
the self-confidence they once had to prescribe and proscribe.
"Youth" belongs to the youth culture, a huge and prosperous
new market not likely to disappear overnight, if ever. Moreover, youth culture has outgrowths. The counter-culture is
one, although my own inclination is to think of it as small
and therefore influential mainly as a "ginger group" to the
mass media. Certainly avant-garde movies, or real revolutionary movies like Ice (revolutionary activities in New York),
or latter-day Jean-Luc Godard movies (readings from Chairman Mao) have not been hits. The other outgrowth of the
youth culture is a sort of upward seepage. People retain
longer the tastes developed when they were youths and those
no longer youthful look to the youth culture for vitality and
excitement. Rock music and the movies are the biggest
items in this seepage.

A minor technological footnote deserves to be added
at this point as we round out the discussion of whether the
new position of movies as a social phenomenon is temporary
or not. This is that as costs escalate in the movie industry,
technology goes on getting relatively cheaper, smaller and
simpler. It is now easier and cheaper for one person to use
substandard equipment that will allow him to make profession-
al-type movies than ever it was before. So more and more
amateur and semi-professional movies are entering the commercial market (Ice, Night of the Living Dead, Is There Sex
After Death?, The Texas Chainsaw Massacre).

So far, then, I have argued that changes in the industry and in the audience and changes going on in the wider
society all indicate that the present situation will continue
for some time with only occasional minor adjustments. I
have not dealt with any countervailing argument other than
the pendulum theory. Perhaps the one I should deal with at
this point is the argument from television. Is it not to be
expected that as television stations proliferate, as cassette

videotape technology improves and libraries of old movies become cheaply available, as a home videotape machine becomes as common as a home-movie camera, there will be further dislocation and inroads into the movies, until they become really no more important than film strips or slide projection?

The Contrast with Television

In fine, my argument will be that network television, feared as it is by politicians, and hence, dominated as it is by bureaucracies and concepts of balance, will never become a vehicle for cultural protest.[3] With cable television, local programming, and workshop television I am not so sure. It is to be expected that the movie industry will not be able to revert to its old ways. The old structures in which its old ways were carried on, the old studio system and the concentration of the industry in Los Angeles, have all crumbled beyond repair. Moreover, television, however unsatisfactory, has become a dominant entertainment medium and will never again allow movies to recapture their preeminent position. But neither the movie medium nor the film industry is dead. Far from it. As long as there are the immense profits to be made which are made every year from the something like a dozen successful films that really hit the social nerve, films will go on being made. As long as movies are an unrivaled medium for capturing the attention of a group of the population for a dramatic story, people will want to go on making them. Unlike television viewing, which takes place in homes with only small groups of watchers, or reading, which is usually a solitary activity, movie-going is a shared group experience which creates a strong empathy among those that have shared it.[4] The advent of a new technology of home cassettes and so on might create new markets for movies, but they will not displace the fundamental theatrical market--although it might be transformed in some way. Indeed, we may expect that more movies will be getting made than ever before. It is certainly true that in Britain and the United States at this moment more movies are being made than ever before. Not perhaps so many commercial movies but a great deal of amateur or semi-amateur movies. That is, movies made by ambitious young people who want to be filmmakers. Sometimes they want to break into the commercial industry, sometimes they do not. As equipment gets lighter and more simple and as costs go down this tendency can be expected to increase and we may eventually see the best of these films going into the theaters.

Movies have room to spare for young people. Television belongs irremediably to the adults. [5] The products of the television medium are transitory--shown once or twice on reruns and at unpredictable and perhaps inconvenient times. As a medium it is hugely expensive because both the making of the videotape, the renting of the transmission facilities and of network time are enormous operations. [6] It is a medium for the home and the family and hence has to keep its eye on the lowest common denominator (or least offensive denominator)[7] not only in the sense that it experiments rarely, which is true, but also in that the values it endorses are irremediably those of respectable bourgeois people. This is not because of a conspiracy on the part of the people making television, but because it is almost impossible for television to preselect its audience, to aim deliberately at a subculture. Television has yet to develop anything like the FM radio stations which concentrate on serious music or intellectual matter, or experimental radio which offends no one because people know what will be on those stations and hence need not tune them in. Television is still too general and expensive a medium to have achieved this. Sooner or later, we may expect youth television stations and perhaps even a youth network to arise. But, meanwhile, the situation being as it is, there is room for a medium for youth and film is that medium. So, far from movies being on the decline, they are on a steadily rising curve and are becoming a respectable part of the culture of the wider society.

However, some of the attitudes that are taken towards movies by this new movie generation are quite different from those of previous ones. Whereas to those of my generation now in their thirties the movies unrolled on the screen in sequence a couple of times a week and were generally a somewhat remote phenomenon peopled with stars, glamorous locations and a general mystery; the medium now is one that most teenagers have mastered either through their home-movie cameras or through courses at high school--and later university, if it comes to that. One can't go onto a campus these days without finding cameras poking out from every doorway. Movies have ceased to have stars in the way that they used to have. Those who act in movies and are made famous by them seem to live in a far less pretentious manner and to be far less harassed and glamorized by their fans than previously. Moreover, this new movie generation has not had great numbers of movies unrolled before them; it has not sat in cheap seats three or four times a week seeing double, triple and quadruple feature programs of everything from appalling B picture trash to Continental masterpieces. On the contrary, the knowledge of the history of the cinema, and its achievements, both by countries and by range of time, is very meager. One might even declare college students of film filmically illiterate. This is not necessarily correlated with effort, although certainly it is difficult even for a devotee to catch up on the history of the film now because of the sheer bulk of the backlog. Many countries have a film theater connected with a national film museum where classics of the screen are mounted periodically. But a great deal of traveling and digging in archives and hence money has to be invested to do all this. Film historians of my generation are still staggering around the archives discovering "entertainment" films made in the United States in the twenties and thirties which are of considerable quality and which somehow have been overlooked and buried for years, thought to be lost, and so on.

Moreover, the principal means available to the present generation for alleviating their film illiteracy is bleary hours with the television late late shows. And, as we noted earlier, Pauline Kael has very plausibly argued in her "Movies on Television" (1968) that seeing movies in a continuous stream and in the indistinct medium of a television screen is not a substitute for seeing them under rather more regularly spaced controls, in cinemas, with a responsive audience and with some coherent relation to the time they were made and order in which they were made. Two important factors in viewing a film are its perceived relation to what is going on in the society at the time; and the perceived relation of movies to each other, especially over time. One movie will influence another. One way of doing a story, even a certain kind of story, will spawn many copies and imitations--some better than the original. One style of comedy or even one style of hero will suddenly proliferate from film to film. The whole cycle of spy and spy-spoof films initiated in 1963 by the James Bond series beginning with Dr. No (Chinese criminal mastermind seeks to control the world) is an example.

Television consumes movies, jumbles them up, dims what visual qualities they may have, miniaturizes what maybe should be grand, trims the image, trims the odd scene and inserts horrid, distracting commercials. Movies available at a flick of the switch are in a way too effortlessly obtained to capture the occasion of their intended viewing situation. The anticipation, the discussion is lost--the audience for television is detached in a way the movie audience was not. Television flows by like a parade, is a weak not a strong medium. It will never replace movies.

An Unsolved Problem: Racism

Before ending this short book I want to return to its major theme, bring up some unanswered questions, produce some new information, and qualify an impression that earlier argumentation may have given. First the qualification: if I have spoken out in favor of the American commercial movie it is because it is so often derided. If I have claimed status for it as a document, that is because this was so long denied it. But if I have suggested the American movie bore a more interesting and critical relationship to American society than it has been credited with, it is time now to qualify. One huge failure in the American commercial movie has been its attitude toward black people. There has been an invisibility about the Negro and his monstrous treatment that comes through both in the rarity of blacks on the screen, and in the way they are portrayed when they do make an appearance.

Hollywood was tasked with this neglect long ago, by the NAACP and others. Why were Negroes always loyal servants, entertainers or "darky" clowns (Bogle 1973)? The reply was often that 30 per cent of theaters were in the South and that Southern audiences would not tolerate films sympathetic to the black. A young social historian, Thomas Cripps (1971), has exploded this argument. He shows that Southern box-office receipts were much smaller a percentage of nationwide receipts than the numbers of Southern theaters would suggest, and that there is ample evidence that Southern audiences (of both races) would accept movies on race themes. So eager were Negro audiences that enterprising blacks were able to create "ghetto" or "race" films for showing exclusively in black neighborhoods. Made quite independently of Hollywood, with all-Negro talent, these films are of some interest as documents since they reveal that blacks were not without their own unconscious racial bias (Leab 1975a).

Cripps concludes that the argument from the Southern box office was a subterfuge designed to justify the racism of Hollywood. While I am sure Hollywood participated in the racism that was widespread in America in its heyday, Cripps' argument strikes me as a non sequitur. Hollywood may have been afraid of the race issue, but much more important to it was the fact that with so many profitable films to be made, why risk making any that could cause controversy? The only controversy Hollywood was interested in was commercial controversy: sensationalism. Thus Intruder in the Dust (1949) about lynching, Home of the Brave (1949) about psychosis, Pinky (1949) about "passing," along with all-Negro musicals Stormy Weather (1942), Cabin in the Sky (1943), Carmen Jones (1954), and Porgy and Bess (1959) did get made. These were movie topics which, while escaping censorship or boycott, nevertheless created enough stir to generate free publicity. With blacks constituting only ten per cent of the population (but, because of poverty, less than 10 per cent of the potential audience), with Southern censor boards so powerful, why take the risk?

Nevertheless, Hollywood's racism was real enough. Racial stereotyping was clearly in evidence in films before Birth of a Nation (the heroic South loses the Civil War) was released in 1915. Cripps contends, however, that Negroes were often treated in a straightforward way (1971). The blatant racism of The Birth of a Nation was something new. This film provoked intense efforts by Negro groups in Boston and New York to get it banned. It was cut, but it was banned in very few cities, despite a riot in Boston. Film historians are inclined to think its cheap romanticization of the South was the beginning of the many films which portrayed the "country" Southern gentry and their happy slaves fighting for honor. The climax came in 1939 when Gone with the Wind (romance against a Southern Civil War background) became the all-time box-office champion despite its pro-South attitudes. Certainly after Birth of a Nation racial stereotyping became routine and blatant (Cripps 1967, 1977, Mapp 1972, Bogle 1973, Leab 1975b).

Until the Second World War blacks appeared in films either as entertainers (usually playing themselves) or in a series of stereotypes: mammy, wide-eyed dummy, servant, railway porter, etc. Negroes were almost never central characters. Stepin Fetchit, Bojangles Robinson, "Rochester" Anderson built careers in small parts. Wars change expectations, victorious wars raise expectations. Segregation in the American armed forces was abolished in 1948. After the war there was a cycle of Negro "problem" films. Blacks became central characters, but only because they were blacks. The films were about the race problem. Both Pinky and Lost Boundaries (1949) were about "passing." In Pinky a white

Negress with a black mother returns home to the South and struggles with the problem of identity (cf. Imitation of Life); Lost Boundaries shows the strain on a light-skinned Negro doctor who passes for white in a small New England town. Intruder in the Dust (helping an unjustly accused black), Home of the Brave (curing a Negro soldier sent out of his mind by prejudice), No Way Out (prejudice nearly wrecks Negro internist's career, 1950), and Black Like Me (journalist dons blackface to see what prejudice is like, 1964) are titles hardly needing exegesis. Suffice it to say, love and understanding usually won through against prejudice and fear. People came to terms with things as they were. The institutional supports of racism and its causes were not themes in these problem films. I can recall no war film which made it clear that segregation still existed in the United States Army during World War II.

Before carrying the story of the presentation of blacks in films up to the present, we need to dispel any too naive views about the social psychology of stereotyping and racism. All too often it is simply assumed that these are "bad" aspects of the American past which have faded away in the enlightened present. This is not so; we think it so only because the stereotypes of previous times are often strange to us, and hence easy to spot. We must guard against the assumption that because our present stereotypes are invisible to many we do not operate with any.

Stereotyping is not just a "bad thing" which somehow inflicted itself on less enlightened ages. Were it that, it would be easy to get rid of it. Stereotyping is a special case of the phenomenon we have earlier called "conventions"-- on which all popular art relies heavily. The difference is that "stereotyping" and "racism" are pejorative words, whereas "convention" is neutral. More significant, racial stereotyping is pernicious partly because it is quite unconscious-- rarely is there any intention to slur. Thus one is trying to describe and perhaps prevent something film makers don't necessarily realize they are trading in, and audiences don't necessarily realize they are being sold. So how, then, does it come about? What is the social psychology of racial stereotyping?

We have maintained in this book that movies are not, for the social psychologist, best thought of as simple, describable events "out there" in the external world. Tables and chairs may for certain purposes be taken like that, and even cans of film, but not movies and movie audiences. Rather, movies are better understood as events experienced in a collectively pre-structured perceptual field, idiosyncratic to social groups rather than to single individuals. When we detect and draw attention to stereotyping, then, we are describing a structural feature of the collective perceptual field, which may be "invisible" to the actors. We are applying a reality principle and saying some films "get across" by means of unstated conventions which are pernicious, and they are pernicious mainly because they are untrue. That they are untrue is what the social psychologist claims to know. But is only the social psychologist so privileged--do or did their black victims find them untrue; do or did white audiences find them untrue?

For a start, did Negroes accept their own stereotype in movies? The evidence tells both ways. On general principle we would expect people to repudiate stereotypes which demean them. Specifically, there is evidence that Negroes took no special notice of the slur in the way they were portrayed. Just the fact that there were black-made films about Negroes, shown in ghetto movie houses, indicates their readiness to see themselves other than Hollywood would have them; examination of the content of the actual films reveals strong traces of self-stereotyping (Baldwin 1976, Maynard 1974).

Much of the burden of the "black is beautiful" argument has been that Negroes too often came to see themselves as others see them; entertainers performed and audiences defined their expectations in terms of stereotypes handed down by the white majority. It would be simplistic to say that without this acquiesence the stereotyping could not have gone on; black self-disgust was not a prerequisite. The NAACP protested about racial slurs in films for decades, without the slightest effect. Yet it is true that when the movement for Negro equality began to gather real political, legal and moral force in the 1950s, an increasing sensitivity to stereotyping became apparent, black consciousness developed, and black complaints began to be heard.

Even more interesting, did the white majority accept the stereotyping of blacks? In the racist reality of a solidly segregated society, such as the South was until the 1950s, was the stereotype of Negroes in films a reflection of their reality (as it appeared to the white majority) or a fantasy (how the white majority wished they were)?

Presumably we must distinguish several things here. (1) Things the way they really are for blacks. [8] (2) The way blacks typically perceive their own situation. (3) The way whites perceive the blacks' situation. (4) The way blacks see the stereotyping. (5) The way whites see the stereotyping. For the sake of argument we assume that there is a (1). Clearly, (1) interacts with (2), and (2) interacts with (4). Moreover, (1) with a time qualifier $(1)_{t1}$ might well be different from $(1)_{t2}$. Hence, for the same stereotyping (say, Birth of a Nation--scheming mulattoes and lustful blacks) there may be many equations: $(1)_{t1} \longrightarrow (2)_{t1} \longrightarrow (4)_{t1} \longrightarrow (1)_{t2} \longrightarrow (2)_{t2} \longrightarrow (4)_{t2}$ etc. The point is, that the time numbers run parallel. How 1970s blacks see Birth of a Nation (racist romanticization of the Old South and the Ku Klux Klan) will be a partial function of how they see their situation now (part of which will be how they view their past), and this in turn will be a partial function of how things really are.

The structuring of the perceived social world goes on over time but is never a blank waiting to be filled. If we are all now highly sensitized to the racial stereotypes and slurs of Birth of a Nation and much later Hollywood product as well (e.g., Gone with the Wind), we are presumably different in that regard from those who made the films, who may not themselves have been aware that they were trading in stereotypes at all. Whence indeed do stereotypes come from? A stereotype is like a cartoon--it uses crude and obvious features to capture a resemblance. When the resemblance is social, the features those of a group, one may seek significance in those features singled out and accepted as recognizable. Birth of a Nation (free Negroes are a menace) cannot be the sort of Cleopatra's Nose of racism in movies that Cripps (1963) claims it to be (the interpretation of world history cannot be turned by the simple fact that Cleopatra was beautiful and not ugly). The stereotype of lazy, lustful, good-for-nothing, uppity blacks and mulattoes in that film neither came out of thin air, nor had an inherent power to impose itself on many subsequent Hollywood movies. Indeed, the storm of controversy which Griffith's film aroused might well have warned shrewd businessmen to beware of racial slurs. Certainly, in no subsequent films that I can recall were Negroes overtly reviled or attacked, as in Griffith's film. Instead, it was the American Indians who came in for a dose of slander. It is far more likely, it seems to me, that the social position of blacks was changing: they were drifting north to the cities, forming an urban subproletariat in competition with the white proletariat, who often perceived them as posing something of a threat. How appropriate then that instead of vicious caricatures of danger- ous Negroes in the 1915 Birth of a Nation, blacks in movies sink to a small and insignificant background image of harm- less fools, devoted servants, credulous and rather simple folk. Likeable and harmless, you see, good for a laugh, basically loyal and content, needing a bit of looking after but nothing to worry about at all.

Stereotyping, then, can be interpreted as basically a defense against imagined and real threats. For this purpose of defense, overt propaganda may be created. But, whereas anti-Semitic stereotyping in Germany in the nineteen-thirties was consciously undertaken by propagandists and the like, the stereotyping in popular Hollywood films is unconscious and therefore more sociologically interesting. We might ex- pect that when conditions further change, the first noticeable thing will be the incorporation of less harmless, even per- haps admirable features into the stereotype. And sure e- nough, we find alleged race-wide black virtues of patience, gentleness, and religion admitted in the 1940s. Following that we get some attempt to look at black sexuality (1950s and to date).

During the fifties, Negro actors like Harry Belafonte, Sidney Poitier and, to a lesser extent, Sammy Davis, Jr., began to emerge as stars (we still await a female star their equal in stature). 9 The trouble was, in every film they were present because of their race. Race rather than character is the protagonist in the drama. Belafonte's main films il- lustrate this well: Carmen Jones (all-black tale of crime passionelle); Island in the Sun (interracial tensions and pas- sions on Jamaica); Odds Against Tomorrow (a superbly plan- ned robbery goes awry partly because of racial prejudice); The World, the Flesh and the Devil (can race prejudice con- tinue when atomic war has left alive only a white woman, a white man and a black man?). Sidney Poitier built an even more successful career in the same way. But in his films there is a tendency for him to become the superspade figure-- noble, intelligent, cultivated, humane and virtually fault-free. Blacks rightly argue that this is a form of emasculation. Look at a selection of his roles: No Way Out (the intern is a victim of bigotry); Blackboard Jungle (one of the few decent pupils in a high school apparently bursting with juvenile de- linquents, 1955); Edge of the City (budding black-white friend- ship is destroyed by prejudice); The Defiant Ones (handcuffed escaped convicts can only succeed if they overcome their mu-

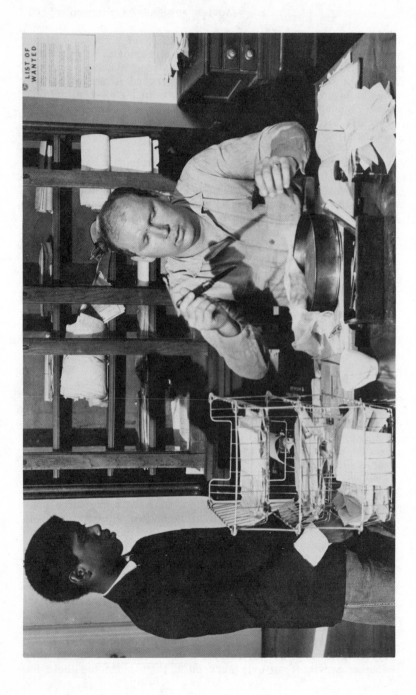

tual prejudice, 1958); Virgin Island (simple black Caribbean
fisherman helps white couple to live on remote island, 1959);
Raisin in the Sun (black Chicago family tries to move into
white neighborhood, 1961); Pressure Point (black psychiatrist
tries to treat young white fascist, 1962); Lillies of the Field
(black handyman helps foreign nuns build church and teaches
them English, 1963); A Patch of Blue (black man helps educate a young blind white woman and they fall in love, he
makes her wait before considering marriage, 1965); The Slen-
der Thread (suicide being talked down by telephone does not
know his helper is black, 1965); To Sir with Love (hard to
be a black schoolteacher in an English school, 1967); Guess
Who's Coming to Dinner (black fiancé of white girl announces
marriage is off if either set of parents objects, 1967); In the
Heat of the Night (ace black Philadelphia detective shows
Southern red necks how to solve a murder, 1967); They Call
Me Mister Tibbs (1970), The Organization (further adventures
of the Philadelphia detective, 1971); Brother John (the Messiah
has returned and he is black, 1972).

Poitier himself realized that he was getting improbably
perfect blacks to play, and began a one-man campaign to
break what had come to seem an equally dehumanizing liberal
stereotype that all blacks are wonderful. The first results
were For Love of Ivy (black criminal sleeps with black maid
then reforms, 1968); and Buck and the Preacher (outlaw and
fake preacher team up in the West, 1972).

It is, then, only in the 1970s that we have seen movies even begin to show blacks as an integral and normal part
of American society, allowing that the bulk of them are poor,
some are criminal, and some are well-educated and respectable, as well as colorful and witty. At all events these films
allow that blacks are there, simply as part of America, and
not because they are blacks. As various writers have put it
(Cripps 1967, Moss 1963, Mapp 1970), the insulting Rastus
image and the flattering "supernigger" image have this much
in common: they are unreal. The black is a person much
like any one else and movies will in a crucial way not be

Opposite: William H. Armstrong's novel-made-movie Sounder
(1972), 20th Century-Fox), adapted by Lonne Elder III, was
a strong attempt to present black experience in a rounded
way. Most of the people in the film are black, and all the
blacks are people--a triumph for white director Martin Ritt.
Here the sheriff (James Best) is suspicious of a cake David
(Kevin Hooks) has brought for his father.

true to our society until this realization informs them as a matter of course. America has to bring her official liberal ideology into practice in her institutions, like movies.

It is to be hoped that the recent wave of black-orientated movies will lead to something. Watermelon Man (comic troubles of a white man who turns black overnight, 1970); Sweet Sweetback's Baaadass Song (docile black turns violent under intolerable provocation and lams out to Mexico); Cotton Comes to Harlem (1970) and Come Back Charleston Blue (1972), adventures of Chester Himes' two black policemen; Shaft (1971), Shaft's Big Score (1972), and Shaft in Africa (1973) (black private eye gets the better of whitey and bestows sexual favors generously on girls of all colors); Superfly (dope dealing, 1972); Cool Breeze (remake of The Asphalt Jungle with an all-black cast, 1972); Black Gunn (black private eye, 1972); and Blacula (black vampire, 1972) all are examples. In these films blacks are heroes, but they are also smart, unscrupulous and lecherous. Perhaps this new run of movies will have a cathartic effect and the public will become bored with these exaggerated positive stereotypes and come to accept black characters who are included not simply in order to let the film explore some aspect of the race problem. The problem film is a cop-out way of "dealing" with blacks, or any other aspect of society, as the producers of the failed films of the student rebellion film cycle found out; and as the producers of the predicatable but yet to be made Women's Liberation cycle will find out too.

So far, the route to the integration of blacks and black content has been choppy. Slavery, the South, and prejudice, still seem to attract filmmakers the most. Burn! (1968) was an unrelenting portrait of the mistreatment of blacks on a Caribbean island in the eighteenth century. Hurry Sundown (1967), Mandingo (1975) and Drum (1976) are tales of the sweaty Southland. Lady Sings the Blues (1972) ushered in the latest bid of a black songstress for movie stardom (Diana Ross plays Billie Holiday). Martin Ritt, a director of strong liberal sympathies, realized two fairly well integrated pictures, The Great White Hope (1970) about a black boxer and his white mistress and Sounder (1972), a story of a family of sharecroppers.

In the matter of such society-wide problems as racism, films can be of the greatest service as well as of the greatest entertainment, for there are clear areas where films can help in anticipatory socialization and learning. The properly equal and humanized black man and woman does not need discussion, they need showing. Not as a problem, but as a fact. On this subject Hollywood's protest, "If you want to send a message, call Western Union," will not do. Movies can constitute a useful protest on behalf of black people simply by humanizing them. Even if films have no influence on their audiences at all, society has some right to demand this response of movies. Laws, and arguments are one thing; basic human attitudes are another. It is not until attitudes change that the hundred and one small slights and insults to which blacks are subjected will cease. One would be naive to believe that all stereotyping can be erased, but some can be done without. Movies can be a model of the acceptance of integration--an example even if they are not followed. Movies can be a positive influence, I am sure, and the black is a case where it is about time they got a bit ahead of the society instead of being behind for over eighty years.

It is, however, possible that television has taken over and made its own this particular subject. The first impact was the long film The Autobiography of Miss Jane Pitman (1973). Supposedly the reminiscences of a 110-year-old black woman, this film was a panorama of black history since the Civil War. Beginning with the problem of integration in 1962, it has its central character look back in a sort of "you've come a long way, baby" spirit. This is not to suggest that John Korty's film (from Ernest J. Gaines' novel) wasn't well and judiciously made. Indeed, its length and concentration were only possible because it was made for television.

What succeeded it was even more remarkable; I refer to Roots. Early in 1977, the ABC Television network screened, on eight successive nights, a mini-series adaptation of Alex Haley's runaway best-seller, Roots. Audience research (according to Time, February 14, 1977) indicates that this program reached the largest audience ever for a television show; over 130 million people saw some part of it, and over 80 million watched the last episode. Roots is not arrière-garde (like Gone With the Wind, the previous holder of the audience record), no more is it avant-garde. It is, as television is, middle of the road. Its theme is family and history; we are what we come from. Like much of television, the program uses melodramatic clichés, drawn from movies and from daytime soap opera. But it is also invested with strongly mythic overtones. Apparently, for many viewers, it crystallized black history in a way both black and white viewers wish to see it. To point out in criticism of it that

it is institutions and conditions which mold people, that history is not an explanation of the present, may seem spoilsportish. Perhaps it is. Perhaps Roots will alter attitudes. Perhaps whites will find the guilt it engenders cleansing, perhaps blacks will find their anger canalized. If so, it may assist that change of heart that Lyndon Johnson declared a sine qua non of black emancipation.

It will be interesting to see what influence these television events will have on movies.

NOTES

1. See the important studies by Himmelweit, Oppenheim and Vince (1958) in Britain, and by Schramm, Lyle and Parker (1961) in the United States: both conducted elaborate research but could come up with virtually nothing negative. The recent report on violence by the U.S. Surgeon General was the first to claim some effect.

2. Although it is entirely arguable whether they are seen by anything like the number of people who would have seen an older hit like Gone with the Wind (Southern belle Scarlett meets her match in Southern rascal Rhett).

3. Robin Day, "Troubled Reflections of a TV Journalist," Encounter, vol. 34, 1970, May, pp. 78-88; Anthony Jay, Sunday Times, 19 November 1972, argue that inherent limitations in the way the medium itself operates also reinforce this point.

4. Discussing a television program with someone lacks much of the vividness and clarity of doing the same to a movie.

Opposite: A formula for films with black-appeal in the seventies became: take a genre (private eye, horror), make the main character, and several others black, add/ sex and action, shake and sell. Chuck Bail's Cleopatra Jones and the Casino of Gold (1975) brought together Warner Brothers and Run Run Shaw to film blackness + sex + spy + female kung fu = no great success. Perhaps in this confrontation Tamara Dobson (seated at left, as Cleopatra Jones), Tien Nee (seated at center, as Mi Ling) and Stella Stevens (standing, as Dragon Lady) are wondering why not all formulas succeed.

5. Les Brown adds the pediatric and geriatric ends of the population.

6. Garth Jowett rightly points out, however, that the cost per thousand delivery of the television audience is much lower than any other medium, especially the commercial film.

7. See Les Brown (1971).

8. Again, "really are" to whom? Some supposedly detached or neutral observer? Whence? Mars perhaps? There is no privileged vantage point.

9. Eartha Kitt, like Lena Horne and Dorothy Danbridge before her, never became a superstar. Whether Diana Ross will succeed remains to be seen.

BIBLIOGRAPHY

Adler, Mortimer, 1937, Art and Prudence, Chicago: University of Chicago.

Adorno, T. W., 1941, "On Popular Music," Studies in Philosophy and Social Science, vol. 9, pp. 17-47.

_____, 1950, The Authoritarian Personality, New York: Harper.

_____, 1954, "How to Look at Television," Quarterly of Film, Radio and Television, vol. 8, pp. 213-36.

Albert, R. S., 1957, "The Role of Mass Media and the Effect of Aggressive Film Content Upon Children's Aggressive Response and Identification Choices," Genetic Psychology Monographs, vol. 55, pp. 211-85.

Allsop, Kenneth, 1958, The Angry Decade, London: Hutchinson.

Arnheim, Rudolf, 1943, "The World of the Daytime Serial," in Lazarsfeld and Stanton, pp. 507-48.

Baldwin, James, 1976, The Devil Finds Work, New York: The Dial Press.

Bandura, Albert; Ross, D.; and Ross, S. A., 1963, "Imitation of Film-Mediated Aggressive Models," Journal of Abnormal and Social Psychology, vol. 66, pp. 3-11.

Bauer, Raymond, 1958, "The Communicator and the Audience," Journal of Conflict Resolution, vol. 2, pp. 67-77.

_____, 1963, "The Obstinate Audience," American Psychologist, vol. 19, pp. 319-28.

Bauer, Raymond, and Bauer, A., 1960, "America, Mass Society and Mass Media," Journal of Social Issues, vol. 16, pp. 3-66.
177

Baxter, John, 1972, Hollywood in the Sixties, New York: Barnes.

Berelson, Bernard, 1961, "The Great Debate on Cultural Democracy," Studies in Public Communication, vol. 3, pp. 3-14.

Bergman, Andrew, 1971, We're in the Money, New York: New York University Press.

Berkowitz, Leonard, 1962, Aggression: A Social Psychological Analysis, New York: McGraw Hill.

Blanchard, Phyllis, 1928, Child and Society, New York: Longmans, Green.

Bluem, A. William, and Squire, Jason E., 1972, The Movie Business, New York: Hastings House.

Bogle, Donald, 1973, Toms, Coons, Mulattoes, Mammies, and Bucks, New York: Viking Press.

Brodbeck, A. J., 1955, "The Mass Media as Socializing Agents," paper read to the American Psychological Association, San Francisco, September 1955. Available in mimeograph from the author.

Brogan, D. W., 1954, "The Problem of High Culture and Mass Culture," Diogenes, vol. 5, pp. 1-13.

Brown, Les, 1971, Television: The Business Behind the Box, New York: Harcourt Brace Jovanovich.

Brown, Roger, 1965, Social Psychology, Glencoe, N. Y.: Free Press.

Carnegie, Andrew, 1917, The Empire of Business, Garden City:

Carnegie, Dale, 1936, How to Win Friends and Influence People, New York: Simon and Schuster.

Carter, Everett, 1960, "Cultural History Written with Lightning: The Significance of The Birth of a Nation," American Quarterly, vol. 12, pp. 347-57.

Cooper, Eunice, and Jahoda, Marie, 1947, "The Evasion of

Propaganda," Journal of Psychology, vol. 23, pp. 15-25.

_____, and Dinerman, Helen, 1951, "Analysis of the Film Don't Be a Sucker: A Study in Communication," Public Opinion Quarterly, vol. 14, pp. 234-64.

Cripps, Thomas, 1963, "The Negro Reaction to the Motion Picture 'Birth of a Nation'," Historian, vol. 23, pp. 344-62.

_____, 1967, "The Death of Rastus: Negroes in American Films Since 1945," Phylon, vol. 28, pp. 267-75.

_____, 1970, "The Myth of the Southern Box Office: Factors in the Perpetuation of White Supremacy in Films 1920-40," in James C. Curtis and Lewis L. Gould, eds., The Black Experience in America: Selected Essays, Austin: University of Texas Press, pp. 116-44.

_____, 1977, Slow Fade to Black, New York: Oxford University Press.

Danziger, Kurt, 1971, Socialization, Harmondsworth, England: Penguin Books.

Day, Robin, 1970, "Troubled Reflections of a TV Journalist," Encounter, vol. 34, May, pp. 78-88.

Deming, Barbara, 1969, Running Away from Myself, New York: Grossman.

Dowdy, Andrew, 1973, Movies Are Better Than Ever, New York: William Morrow

Dunne, John Gregory, 1969, The Studio, New York: Farrar, Straus & Giroux.

Durgnat, Raymond, 1969, The Crazy Mirror, London: Faber and Faber.

Elkin, Fred, 1949, "God, Radio and the Movies," Hollywood Quarterly, vol. 5, pp. 105-14.

_____, 1954, "The Value Implications of Popular Films," Sociology and Social Research, vol. 38, pp. 320-2.

_____, 1955, "Popular Hero Symbols and Audience Gratifications," Journal of Educational Psychology, vol. 29, pp. 97-107.

Fearing, Franklin, 1947, "Influence of the Movies on Attitudes and Behavior," Annals of the American Academy of Political and Social Science, vol. 254, "The Motion Picture Industry," ed. by G. S. Watkins, pp. 70-9.

_____, 1950, Motion Pictures as a Medium of Instruction and Communication, Berkeley: University of California Press.

_____, 1953, "Towards a Psychological Theory of Human Communication," Journal of Personality, vol. 22, pp. 71-88.

Festinger, Leon, 1957, A Theory of Cognitive Dissonance, New York: Row, Peterson.

Forman, H. J., 1933, Our Movie Made Children, New York: Macmillan.

Freud, Sigmund, 1930, Civilization and Its Discontents, London: The Hogarth Press

Gans, Herbert J., 1957, "The Creator-Audience Relationship in the Mass Media: An Analysis of Movie Making," in Rosenberg and White, 1957, pp. 315-324.

_____, 1959, American Films and Television Programs on British Screens, Philadelphia: Institute of Urban Studies, University of Pennsylvania.

_____, 1960, "The Relationship Between the Movies and the Public, and some Implications for Movie Criticism and Movie Making," unpublished.

_____, 1962a, The Urban Villagers, Glencoe, N. Y.: Free Press.

_____, 1962b, "Hollywood Films on British Screens: An Analysis of the Function of American Popular Culture Abroad," Social Problems, vol. 9, pp. 324-8.

_____, 1966, "Popular Culture in America: Social Problems in a Mass Society or Social Asset in a Plural Society?", in H. S. Becker, ed., Social Problems: A Modern Approach, New York: Wiley, pp. 549-620.

_____, 1974, Popular Culture and High Culture, New York: Basic Books.

Geduld, Harry M., and Gottesman, Ronald, eds., 1970, Sergei Eisenstein and Upton Sinclair, Bloomington: Indiana University Press.

Glazer, Nathan, and Moynihan, Daniel P., 1963, Beyond the Melting Pot, Cambridge: Massachusetts Institute of Technology Press.

Goffman, Erving, 1963, Behavior in Public Places, Glencoe, N.Y.: Free Press.

Guback, Thomas H., 1969, The International Film Industry, Bloomington: Indiana University Press.

Hauser, Arnold, 1951, The Social History of Art, London: Routledge and Kegan Paul.

Herzog, Herta, 1943, "What Do We Really Know About Day-Time Serial Listeners?", in Lazarsfeld and Stanton, pp. 3-23.

Higham, Charles, 1970, The Films of Orson Welles, Berkeley: University of California Press.

_____, 1972, Hollywood at Sunset, New York: Saturday Review Press.

_____, and Greenberg, Joel, 1968, Hollywood in the Forties, New York: Barnes.

Hoggart, Richard, 1957, The Uses of Literacy, London: Chatto and Windus.

Horton, Donald, and Wohl, R.R., 1956, "Mass Communication and Parasocial Interaction," Psychiatry, vol. 19, pp. 215-29.

Hovland, Carl I.; Lumsdaine, A.A.; and Sheffield, F.D., 1949, Experiments in Mass Communication, Princeton, N.J.: Princeton University Press.

Howe, A.H., 1965, "A Banker Looks at the Picture Business," The Journal of the Screen Producer's Guild, December, 9-16.

_____, 1972, "Bankers and Movie Makers," in Bluem and Squire, pp. 57-67.

Huaco, George, 1965, The Sociology of Film Art, New York: Basic Books.

Iverson, William, 1964, "The Pious Pornographers Revisited," Playboy, vol. 11, September, pp. 92-6, 190-99; October pp. 116-8, 202-18.

Jacobs, Lewis, 1939, The Rise of the American Film, New York: Harcourt Brace.

Jarvie, I. C., 1970, Movies and Society, New York: Basic Books.

_____, 1972, Concepts and Society, London: Routledge.

_____, 1978, "Seeing Through Movies," Philosophy of the Social Sciences, vol. 8, forthcoming.

Jones, Dorothy, 1942, "Quantitative Analysis of Motion Picture Content," Public Opinion Quarterly, vol. 6, pp. 411-28.

_____, 1945, "The Hollywood War Film: 1942-44," Hollywood Quarterly, vol. 1, pp. 1-19.

_____, 1950, "Quantitative Analysis of Motion Picture Content," Public Opinion Quarterly, vol. 14, pp. 554-8.

_____, 1955, The Portrayal of China and India on the American Screen 1896-1955, Cambridge: Massachusetts Institute of Technology Press.

Jowett, Garth, 1972, "Media Power and Social Control: The Motion Picture in America, 1894-1936," Ph.D. thesis, University of Pennsylvania.

_____, 1976, Film: The Democratic Art, Boston: Little, Brown.

Kael, Pauline, 1968, "Movies on Television," in Kiss Kiss Bang Bang, Boston: Atlantic-Little, Brown.

Kanfer, Stefan, 1973, A Journal of the Plague Years, New York: Atheneum.

Katz, Elihu, and Lazarsfeld, Paul, 1955, Personal Influence, Glencoe, N.Y.: Free Press.

Klapper, Joseph, 1961, The Effects of Mass Communication, Glencoe, N.Y.: Free Press

Knebel, Fletcher, 1970, "Hollywood: Broke and Getting Rich," Look, vol. 34, November 3, pp. 50-2.

Knight, Arthur, 1970, "A Flood of Film Books," Saturday Review, vol. 53, December 26, pp. 15-17.

Kracauer, Siegfried, 1947, From Caligari to Hitler, Princeton, N.J.: Princeton University Press.

_____, 1950, "National Types as Hollywood Presents Them," Cinema 1950, pp. 140-69.

Lane, Tamar, 1923, What's Wrong with the Movies? Los Angeles: Waverly Co.

Lazarsfeld, Paul, and Stanton, Frank, 1943, Radio Research 1942-43, New York: Duell, Sloane and Pearce.

Leab, Daniel J., 1975a, "A Pale Black Imitation: All-Colored Films: 1930-60," Journal of Popular Film, vol. 4, pp. 56-76.

_____, 1975b, From Sambo to Superspade, Boston: Houghton Mifflin.

Levinger, Larry, 1972, "Shut Up and Show the Movies," Playboy, vol. 19, August, 127-8, 194-8.

Leyda, Jay, 1960, Kino, London: Allen and Unwin.

Longford, The Earl of, 1972, The Longford Report, London: Coronet.

Lovaas, O.I., 1961, "Effect of Exposure to Symbolic Aggression on Aggressive Behavior," Child Development, vol. 32, pp. 37-44.

Lynd, Robert S., and Helen Merrell, 1928, Middletown, New York: Harcourt Brace.

Maccoby, Eleanor, 1964, "The Effects of the Mass Media,"

in M. Hoffman and L. Hoffman, eds. , Review of Child Development Research, New York: Russell Sage Foundation, pp. 323-48.

Macdonald, Dwight, 1954, "A Theory of Mass Culture," Diogenes, vol. 3, pp. 1-17.

McDougall, William, 1923 (15th edition), An Introduction to Social Psychology, Boston: Luce.

Mapp, E. C. , 1970, "The Portrayal of the Negro in American Motion Pictures, 1962-1968," Ph. D. thesis, New York University. [Published in 1971 in major revision covering the silents through 1970 as Blacks in American Films: Today and Yesterday by Edward Mapp, Metuchen, N. J. : Scarecrow Press.]

Marcus, Robert, 1970, "Moviegoing and American Culture," Journal of Popular Culture, vol. 3, pp. 754-66.

Mayer, J. P. , 1946, Sociology of Film, London: Faber and Faber.

_____, 1948, British Cinemas and Their Audiences, London: Dennis Dobson.

_____, 1972, Sociology of Film, reprint with a new Introduction, New York: Arno Press.

Maynard, Richard A. , 1974, The Black Man on Film: Racial Stereotyping, Rochelle Park, N. J. : Hayden Book Co.

Mendelsohn, Harold, 1966, Mass Entertainment, New Haven, Conn. : College and University Press.

Mercillon, Henri, 1953, Cinéma et Monopoles, Paris: Armand Colin.

Mill, John Stuart, 1856 (revised 4th edition), System of Logic, London: Parker.

Mitchell, Alice Miller, 1929, Children and Movies, Chicago: University of Chicago.

Moley, Raymond, 1938, Are We Movie Made? New York: Macy-Masius.

Montagu, Ivor, 1968, With Eisenstein in Hollywood, Berlin: Seven Seas.

Moss, Carlton, 1963, "The Negro in American Films" Freedomways, vol. 3, pp. 134-42.

Munsterberg, Hugo, 1916, The Photoplay: A Psychological Study, New York: D. Appleton and Co.

National Conference on Social Work, Proceedings, Annual.

Oberholtzer, Ellis P., 1922, The Morals of the Movies, Philadelphia: Penn Publishing Co.

Phelan, the Rev. J. J., 1919, Motion Pictures as a Phase of Commercialized Amusement in Toledo, Ohio, Toledo: Little Book Press.

Poffenberger, A. T., 1921, "Motion Pictures and Crime," Scientific Monthly, April, pp. 336-9.

Powdermaker, Hortense, 1950, Hollywood--the Dream Factory, Boston: Little, Brown and Co.

Randall, Richard S., 1968, Censorship of the Movies, Madison: University of Wisconsin Press.

Richards, Jeffrey, 1973, Visions of Yesterday, London: Routledge.

Riesman, David; Glazer, Nathan; and Denny, Reuel, 1950, The Lonely Crowd, New Haven, Conn.; Yale University Press.

Rimberg, John, 1959, "Motion Picture in the Soviet Union 1918-1952: A Sociological Analysis," Ph. D. thesis, Columbia University.

Roberts, John M., and Sutton-Smith, B., 1966, "Cross-Cultural Correlates of Games of Chance," Behavior Science Notes, vol. 1, pp. 131-44.

_____, Arth, M. J. and Bush, R. R., 1959, "Games in Culture," American Anthropologist, vol. 61, pp. 597-605.

Rosenberg, Bernard, and White, David Manning, 1957, Mass Culture, Glencoe, N. Y.: Free Press.

_____, 1971, Mass Culture Revisited, Glencoe, N. Y. : Free Press.

Ross, Lillian, 1952, Picture, New York: Harcourt Brace.

Rosten, Leo, 1941, Hollywood: The Movie Colony, the Movie Makers, New York: Harcourt, Brace and Co.

Schulman, Gary, 1965, "The Two-Step Flow Hypothesis of Mass Communication: A Reformulation Using Cognitive Dissonance Theory," Ph. D. thesis, Stanford University.

Seton, Marie, 1952, Sergei M. Eisenstein, New York: Wyn.

Shils, Edward, 1957, "Daydreams and Nightmares, Reflections on the Criticisms of Mass Culture," Sewanee Review, vol. 65, pp. 587-608.

_____, 1961, "Mass Society and Its Culture," in Norman Jacobs, ed. , Culture for the Millions?, Boston: Beacon Press, pp. 1-27.

Sklar, Robert, 1975, Movie-Made America, New York: Random House.

Smiles, Sam, 1862, Self-Help, London: John Murray.

Smith, Julian, 1975, Looking Away, New York: Scribner's.

Smith, Paul (ed.), 1976, The Historian and the Film, New York: Cambridge University Press.

Soderbergh, Peter, 1970, "Upton Sinclair and Hollywood," Midwest Quarterly, vol. 11, pp. 173-91.

Stephenson, W. , 1967, The Play Theory of Mass Communication, Chicago: University of Chicago Press.

Taylor, John Russell, 1962, Anger and After, London: Methuen.

Trilling, Diana, 1970, "Easy Rider and Its Critics," Atlantic Monthly, vol. 226, September, pp. 90-5; reprinted in Rosenberg and White 1971, pp. 233-244.

Tyler, Parker, 1944, The Hollywood Hallucination, New York: Creative Age Press.

_____, 1947, Magic and Myth of the Movies, New York: Henry Holt and Co.

United States, Commission on Obscenity and Pornography, 1970, The Report, New York: Random House.

_____, Surgeon-General's Scientific Advisory Committee on Television and Social Behavior, 1972, Television and Growing Up: The Impact of Televised Violence, Washington: U. S. G. P. O.

Vardac, Nicholas, 1949, Stage to Screen, Cambridge, Mass.: Harvard University Press.

Warner, W. Lloyd, and Henry, William E., 1948, "The Radio Day Time Serial: A Symbolic Analysis," Genetic Psychology Monographs, vol. 37, pp. 3-71.

Wiese, M., and Cole, S., 1946, "A Study of Children's Attitudes and the Influence of the Commercial Motion Picture," Journal of Psychology, vol. 21, pp. 151-71.

Wilensky, Harold, 1964, "Mass Society and Mass Culture," American Sociological Review, vol. 29, pp. 173-97.

Williams, Raymond, 1958, Culture and Society 1780-1950, New York: Columbia University Press.

Wilson, John, 1961, "Film Illiteracy in Africa," Canadaian Communications, summer, vol. 1, 7-14.

Wolfenstein, Martha, and Leites, Nathan, 1950, Movies: A Psychological Study, Glencoe, N. Y.: Free Press.

Wright, Will, 1975, Six Guns and Society, Berkeley: University of California Press.

INDEX OF NAMES

SUBJECT INDEX

INDEX OF FILMS

The title is followed by the country, date and director's name, given, so far as possible, in accord with Britain's authoritative Monthly Film Bulletin.